# READY

*Heartbreak, Dating & My Journey Toward Love*

Anita love!
Thank you for
believing in me!
& May you appreciate
your LOVE fully!

## Heather Alaine

xoxo H

# DEDICATIONS

To my **mother** and **father** who are celebrating 46 years of marriage. I'm honored by their ongoing love and support. I'm in awe of their wisdom that is typically sprinkled with humor. Note: Their copy of this book contains blacked-out sections on a few topics like a top secret document, per my pop's suggestion.

To my **friends** who have listened, empathized, asked questions, called me on my own issues, offered advice, and loved me absolutely, 100% unconditionally, through beautiful times *and especially* in challenging moments.

To my **editors** for their vital feedback. Handing in drafts was like asking them to wash my intimate apparel.

- **Britt Bravo,** who realized the random dating stories could evolve into a book. For years, she has helped me figure out my next steps in our career consultancy meetings. She's also read more books than anyone I know.
- **Ruthie McGrath,** whose response to my fear of men not wanting to date me for writing this book was, "Taylor Swift has written songs about her exes, and she had no problems

finding dates." She also understands my need for organizing and shopping better than most.

- **Jordana King**, whose fire-y approach to living has inspired me since we met our first year of teaching. Our conversations around our faith in love and life being as it should, always bring me back to my center.
- My big brother, **Brett Paul**, who helped edit when I thought I was done (and wasn't at all!). He has helped shape my life from birth on. I look forward to reading his book one day.
- **Nyere da Silva**, who asks questions and delivers feedback as if it's an art form. She quite literally fine-tooth combed all of the tangles out of the final draft. Our side-by-side journey provides deep comfort and laughter in my life. Her willingness to catch me before falling is unparalleled. She's also the best travel buddy ever.
- **Ali Lawrence and Katherine Rothschild,** who both provided feedback as if words are merely a cloud to float upon. Their openness and enthusiasm around providing another round of edits (who knew it took so much work to make writing seem so simple?!) are so deeply appreciated.
- **Jackie Ato, Karen Wertman, Elizabeth Hernández Pimentel-Gopal and Cathy Fischer** for their eagle eyes on such things as passe versus passé, peak versus pique, and random extra periods. I am so grateful for their willingness to jump in so quickly to help as well as the life reminder to not hesitate to ask for help when you need it.

To my amazing dancing **Hipline** ladies in Oakland, who have worked it out with me while singing and shimmying our way through the ups and downs of life. Y'all are my body and soul therapy! A special shout-out to **Gabriela** and **Samar**, the brave creators of this "Shimmy. Connect. Love." movement.

**Guest Readers** Jachyn Davis, Lorea Russell, Ali Amaro, and Anthea Charles for their time and energy in sharing their thoughts on their experience with the book.

To **Bar César** on Piedmont Avenue for letting me sit in the VIP room for countless hours while ordering a cup of tea and a tapa. To **Shakewell** on Lakeshore Avenue for being my go-to spot for finishing editing — your warmth and open arms are heartwarming. My modern-day "Cheers."

*Author's Note:*
*I want to acknowledge that I could have very easily let this process go on (...*
*and on and on...) by having ten more people proofread to catch any last wee*
*mistakes that may exist, or change the structure of a final sentence, or replace*
*one word for a better one. However, I am choosing to publish it as is. In the*
*spirit of letting go of perfectionism, I accept that mistakes and messy-ness are*
*a part of the process. Like most things in life, right?*

# INTRODUCTION

My name is Heather. I am 37 years old. I am still searching for love.

This book began as an ongoing joke with my girlfriends over cocktails. Every time we met up, there were new, entertaining dating tales to tell. What began as a collection of funny and sometimes bizarre stories evolved into a book about my personal journey. And, while, quite frankly, it scares the shit out of me to put this out there, I have found vulnerability and connection to be two of the most crucial elements to living life more fully and authentically. I am coming to you from this tender place.

I realize that you have your own soundtrack on loving, being hurt, trying again, doubting, trying again and still maintaining a strong belief in love. The songs on our soundtracks and the details of our stories will inevitably differ. **The hope I hold for us, deep within my heart, is that we can relate, overlap, mostly agree, disagree from time to time (it's only natural, Love!), feel deeply, and ultimately learn a tremendous amount about ourselves along the way.** You are the reason that I am sharing. Truly.

Before going any deeper, I'd love to share a few things about myself. Think of it as a quick round of speed dating. Here's my two-minutes worth of info for our four-minute introductory chat:

I like turquoise, tapas and feather earrings. I am an advocate of bright colors, glitter, and meditation. I adore tropical vacations and time to chill on the beach. Black tea is a staple in my life; I drink it like most coffee drinkers do lattes. I love sparkling wine aka "bubbles." I am a fan of *Modern Family*, *The Good Wife* and *Law and Order: SVU* — although I try not to watch the latter, as the violence can get stuck in my brain and I really don't need it in there.

*Woah! I am all over the place. I'm just so excited! Let me take a breath and focus.*

I grew up on and off of a military base in Spain, where my parents were both hard-working teachers. My friends were from everywhere, Puerto Rico to California to France. Growing up as an "Americanita," I spoke primarily English, with some Spanglish thrown in. (Not speaking better Spanish is one of my few regrets in life.) I was very shy when I was younger. (This can occasionally come out still if I'm in a big group of people I don't know.) My family flew back to the U.S. every summer to visit friends and family. It wasn't until I moved stateside for college that I experienced serious culture shock, and came to realize how much the unique experience I had growing up overseas impacted my sense of self and my larger worldview.

With a major in English, and minors in Dance and Women's Studies, I moved from Oregon to San

Francisco, and felt as though I'd come home. I became an elementary school teacher, with a strong focus on equity within education. When I got my Master's in Education a couple of years later, I taught movement and dance in schools. Upon moving to the sunny side of the Bay (Oakland) in 2001, I became a Literacy Specialist for kindergarten and first grade students, and began teaching dance fitness to adults as a side gig.

I'm now a full-time dance fitness instructor, personal trainer, and massage practitioner, who still does literacy work part-time. I'm a lifelong learner who enjoys discovering new things, particularly about the body and the brain. I enjoy nerding out on TED Talks, and I get excited when I get to pick which courses I want to take to renew my Personal Training certificate. Most recently, *The New Rules of Posture* has been rocking my mental playground! I get deep joy and satisfaction from the work I do, because I am able to help facilitate people finding balance and happiness in their lives. I feel very blessed. Extremely blessed, actually.

On the fluffier side, I enjoy reading *US Magazine,* to find out the latest juicy gossip on celebrities. And, I've been known to get sucked into an episode or so of *The Bachelorette.* (If I miss the first one, I can usually stay out of it, which is always what I intend to do.) I realize that these nuggets of juiciness are a bit of a contradiction to the above information; I prefer to view it as being multidimensional. Aren't we all, though?

What else? I love, love, love to laugh. Especially with my family and my girlfriends. I've also had quite a few of my biggest laughs come from those shows where people do silly things (as long as they don't get hurt). I've had some serious belly-aching moments from laughing hella hard at videos of folks flying off treadmills. Have you seen the one with the guy that is checking out a woman, falls, and immediately starts doing push-ups as if that was his plan? Hilarious!

On the other side of the spectrum, I don't get mad often. When I do, it usually comes out as being pissy in parking lots or on the freeway, directed at cars driving under the speed limit in the "fast" lane. (Really, people?)

I also don't cry much as an adult and have wondered why this is the case. I think it's due to some life experiences that have hardened my Cancerian outer shell over time. Though, sad stories can make me cry sometimes. Maybe I need to watch *Titanic* again.

To balance everything, I enjoy sitting by the ocean…

Oops! There goes the buzzer! Our speed date is over. That was so fast! The good news is, it looks like we have a spark or at least enough curiosity that we've both written "yes" on our dating cards to get to know each other better.

A heads-up: we are going to begin this journey with a sad song, a heartache, but I promise there will be many different tracks to my playlist.

The stories in this book are based on real people and events. Names and some details have been changed to protect the (sometimes not-so-) innocent. And, while I'd happily shout my friends' names off mountaintops with love, they are included in this otherwise-known-as category too.

## NO ONE ELSE * AMEL LARRIEUX

"**O**pen your work email now." I am surprised by the fierceness in my voice.

He fumbles with the laptop, which is now angled away from me. My focus suddenly shifts to the sound of each key pounding under his fingers. Then, I realize he is most likely trying to delete evidence. "Now!" I demand again with a sense of urgency that does not sound like me at all.

He picks up the computer, shoulders slightly rounded, muttering, "There's no reason to do this." Something is telling me otherwise.

As he sets the computer on my lap, he looks me directly in the eyes, informing me, "I am not going to stay while you look. There is nothing there for you to find. When you are ready to actually have a conversation about the lack of trust <u>you</u> have in our relationship, you let me know, Heather. I'll be upstairs."

I can't tell if the sadness I detect behind his eyes is due to the fact that he feels bad about lying or because it's evident I no longer trust him. *Is he lying?* Even with my uncertainty, the potential for devastation already sits heavy within my heart. *This cannot be happening.*

I watch him slowly climb the staircase to our bedroom. My heart is beating so loudly it makes my body thud in tandem rhythm that seems to echo with a slight delay. My eyes travel to the computer screen. I begin to scroll through his emails, scanning for anything out of the ordinary.

*Maybe I am being ridiculous? He's been putting so much work into our relationship and assuring me I'm the only one. There can't possibly be more women. The ones I found on his phone he said he never even met up with. Wasn't that three months ago now? We've been going to therapy and taking the right steps to make things better between us. He said those women were just about the attention he was craving. Nothing actually happened. He's trying. Maybe it's just me being uptight. What's my problem anyway? Seriously. Why can't I trust him? I always hold on to past shit. I am sure our rockiness has been hard for him too. I can't let this get to me. I love him. We are going to be just...*

Then, I see it. An email that is different from the others. It is casually titled "Hello" to a woman named Lori. He writes:

Wanna do lunch today?

*Lunch with his coworker seems fine. Heather, let this go. Stop being so suspicious.*

Are you free Thursday night?

*Thursday night? That can't be right. Maybe there is a reason for them getting together for work? Maybe there's a reason I've never even heard of this woman? Maybe?*

I go back to the main messages, and continue scrolling down. I come to an abrupt stop at another email. It is also to Lori. The subject reads: "Let's take a long lunch." I hold my breath as I click on it. Every muscle in my body tenses as I read the chain between them.

Him: Please.

Her: Wouldn't a long lunch be nice? I can imagine what you have in mind. If I had the time to play, I would accept your offer without any hesitation!

Him: Let's plan to have some fun at lunch later this week then. Come on! Make me feel wanted! I keep on asking and you keep saying no. Should I stop asking?

My lungs are aching. I exhale abruptly and hard. The ache remains.

Her: I'm not trying to be mean, I promise! But this week alone I have two job interviews, one presentation, two other job application deadlines, a class to attend and another several hours of studying to do on top of it all. I'm overwhelmed and stressed out. I WISH I was in a position to take you up on the offer!

Him: I understand. I just miss you. If you were trying to avoid me, I just wanted to know. Maybe this Sunday or early next week? Give me a call.

My entire body is awash with undulating waves of heat and cold.

Somehow I manage to stand on shaky legs. I walk up the stairs toward our bedroom, carefully placing one foot at a time on each step. I feel as though I'm moving in slow motion. My body does not seem to belong to me. *How can this be happening?* The laptop jabs sharply into the side of my ribs as I make it to the top of the stairs. *I don't understand.*

He is lying on our bed.

I want to curl up with him, close my eyes, go to sleep, and wake up from this bad dream. I feel trapped within. *This can't be happening.*

I spy his phone in his hands, and am warped back into the moment. In a trembling voice, I ask, "Who is Lori?" barely able to speak the question.

*I need to breathe.*

"A co-worker. Why?" he answers, seemingly unfazed, keeping his eyes on his phone. *How is he so calm? Why am I feeling like I am making up this unnecessary drama right now? I'm not. I'm NOT. I just read his invitation to her. But maybe nothing happened? Maybe I'm just reading into it? NO! I'm so damn gullible.*

Still not looking at me, he repeats, "She's just a co-worker, Heather." The tone in his voice when he says my name sounds slightly accusatory, which does not sit well with me. The internal storm that's been brewing erupts to the surface, pouring out of me. I shout to him, at him, "Oh my god! You have got to be fucking kidding me! I've never heard of this woman, and you are inviting her to go on long lunches because you want to feel wanted? What the FUCK are you doing on those lunches? I cannot believe this!" *Did I not make him feel wanted? Did I not give him enough?*

Still maintaining his calm, he looks up at me and replies, "She is a friend, Heather. There is no reason for you to be upset. She was going through a hard time. I was just offering to help her during lunchtime to pack boxes at her apartment, because she is moving. That's it. There's no reason to get all worked up."

Kindness is one of the attributes that drew me to him nearly two years ago. *Maybe this is true? How can this be true?*

He gets up and walks across the room. "I need to use it," he tells me, as he shuts the door to the attached bathroom. I hear the lock click. We never lock the door.

Dazed, I sit down on the bed and begin to scroll through more emails. *I wish I could make this stop. What am I looking for anyway? This is absurd. I love him. He loves me. That should be enough. Why is this happening? Was I not enough for him? Am I not enough?*

I come across another email to a different woman, Susan.

> Him: Hi there! Are you around this weekend? Wanna have some fun?

> Her: I am pretty busy, but would love to find a time. When are you thinking?

> Him: Would love to meet up on Sunday evening, if you could fit me in? I've been fantasizing about you.

*Wait! That's when he is supposed to be dropping his daughter off, and coming home to me. TO ME. How many times has traffic been bad or he had to work late, when in reality he was meeting up with these women instead? He told me that he never actually met up with any of them. I believed him. I can't believe this. How could I have missed this? AND WHAT IN THE WORLD is he doing in the bathroom, with the door locked? With his phone? Is he erasing more emails?*

I quickly stand up and walk to the bathroom door. "I need you to come out." I tell him, my voice unsteady. A shard of my broken heart is lodged in my throat.

"I'm using the bathroom. Hold on," he replies, with the first hint of panic in his voice.

I go back to sit on our bed. I begin to look through his emails again. There is yet another to a woman named Kari.

*No. Just no.*

Her: What time do you get off today?

Him: 4 p.m. Meet you in the lobby?

Her: Can't wait! I'm feeling feisty.

My shoulders cave inward as if to shield my heart from any further pain. I feel heavy. So heavy. The evidence I've been desperately wanting (and so not wanting) to find to confirm this uneasy feeling inside me is now in my hands. It does not bring me any relief. I feel no comfort. It only validates what my body and intuition have been trying to tell me for months: It's over.

# TRY SLEEPING WITH A BROKEN HEART
## ALICIA KEYS

It's over, and yet there is not a definite end to being in each other's lives. With so many areas of our lives intertwined, we attempt to sort through the mess our relationship has become. The home we shared feels tainted. I have an intense need for space from it and from him. It is too hard to reside somewhere that was safe and loving, that was US. *What happens when the We shifts to just Me?* I move in with my friend Rae and her husband. I am not sleeping much, and barely eating due to the emotional turmoil. She gets me on a schedule so that I am sleeping regularly. She encourages me to eat. Rae even makes my favorite breakfast of cinnamon toast with almond butter and honey with a cup of strong, black tea. Eating, sleeping: the basics easily forgotten in any kind of traumatic event. Thank goodness for Rae.

Everything else stays messy. And painful. And surreal. As though I am living on an alternate plane where I am only connected by routines and motions. A hazy, underwater reality that I don't comprehend. My brain cannot process the vast fracture my insides feel.

*How can I live without him? He's my love. But, I certainly can't be with him. He lied. He cheated. Those are not things that a good relationship can be built on. What do I do? God, my head hurts. My heart hurts. My world feels like it's closing in. I have to breathe. I love him so deeply. I miss him. These feelings don't match. THEY DON'T MATCH. What am I supposed to do? I just want to go back to how it was before. Maybe we can make it work somehow? Maybe we can erase the past, just pretend it never happened? Is that possible? I feel like I'm going crazy. How the hell do I navigate this?*

We go to therapy together and individually. Our communication beyond the therapist's office is limited to email and a few phone conversations. I desperately try to figure out how I can cut him out of my life while my heart seems determined to hold on tight. I cannot let go. I don't want to let go. The image in my head is one of us with his daughter at home, singing at the top of our lungs on the karaoke machine. The feeling that resides in my heart is the pure safety I felt falling asleep next to him on the couch as he watched TV, calmed by his breathing. Feeling the gentle rise and fall of his belly. Listening to his heartbeat. *There has got to be a way to get back to love. His love. Our love.*

Two weeks into our separation feels like an eternity.

I need more clothes, so I drive back to our apartment. My mind is moving quickly, still trying to make sense of what went wrong. *We were on track; one of the later trains to leave the station, but definitely on track. We moved along quickly after we met; he was perfect for me. From the first moment we saw each other, there was a strong attraction, which only grew with time. We laughed. A lot. God, I miss his laugh. And, he was such a gentleman. Even on our first date, although I could tell he wanted more, he kissed my cheek goodnight. Everything felt so good. So right. He was everything I wanted. We made our home together. The only man I ever lived with. We were in the process of talking about having a child together. Geez. Imagine that, a child. We were even thinking of names that we liked. I always adored the name Jasmine. If it was a girl. He was looking at engagement rings. How did we end up here?*

As I pull up to our apartment, I see his car parked in the driveway. I didn't expect him to be home. I am anxiously excited to see him outside of our therapy box. Butterflies in my stomach. Nervous as hell. *Maybe I can push the past aside, and we can still live our happily ever after.*

Upon seeing each other, we immediately hug. We cling to one another. I try to focus solely on the feeling of comfort that comes with being embraced tightly in his arms, his body covering my vulnerable heart. *My love, I have missed you.* My body lets go, softens, with the familiarity of him. Then, I begin to cry. Words begin to escape my mouth about how hard it is without him and how confused I feel. He calms me with his words, caresses my soul with gentleness. He moves forward to kiss me, and I pull away. While I yearn deeply for his loving protection, the contradictory images burned into my mind haunt me in my restless dreams, refusing to be overlooked—him naked, passionate, sharing himself with other women.

Sensing my hesitancy, he suggests that we move to our kitchen table to talk. We have shared many significant conversations and meals over our wooden, rickety Ikea table. This ritual was one of the things I was the most proud of in our home that we shared for almost a year. We sit in momentary silence. The cat runs over to rub on my legs, welcoming me back, perhaps wondering where I've been.

I take a big breath, reminding myself to be brave. *You are grown. You are strong. You need to speak your truth, Heather.* In the past, this would have seemed impossible, as I used to swallow the pain without voicing it. Words begin to cascade out of my mouth again, but this time at such a rate that I cannot even make sense of what I am saying. As my ramble continues, so does my volume. I notice him stand up from the kitchen table, his posture erect. *Why is he standing? Is he upset with me? How can he upset with <u>me</u>?* Things are happening so quickly. My words that I've been toppling over crescendo into accusatory screams. *I wasn't the one who did anything wrong! He lied to me. He cheated.*

Both of my hands slam on the table, acting as exclamation marks to my words. A slightly delayed tingle travels up my arms, into my shoulders, behind my shoulder blades, and finally settles into the shadows behind my heart. It's an uncanny sensation that jolts me back into the moment. Into this moment. Of yelling. Then, a pause. Silence. Having been outwardly expressed, my anger dissipates as if vapor transformed, and I am suddenly overwhelmed by complete and utter sadness that sits solidly at my core, deep in my belly. My anger, however, has ignited his. He steps towards me with his own fire, chest puffed, hand raised. His usually gentle eyes reveal a bitterness I've never seen before. *What? No.* My sadness instantly turns into raw fear. I step back, away from him, away from our relationship, away from any hope that we can ever put the shattered pieces back together again. *I can't.*

Two days later, in our last therapy session, we say good-bye.

I walk out of the therapist's office, beyond thankful that my friend, Yesenia, has agreed to meet me. She catches me as I stumble out the door and embraces me with such love and compassion. Yesenia's support, which comes from her deep empathy of having experienced a similar story of her own, humbles me.

## LOSING MY GROUND * FERGIE

I cry.

Days upon days upon weeks.

A steady waterfall of tears.

I continue to cry.

There is no laughter, no lightheartedness. Just tears. Tears upon tears upon tears.

Weeks turn into a month. Two months. Three months.

Life feels heavy. Unbearable.

My heart is an anchor — submerged, rusted, obsolete, sunken.

And, then, one day, I stop.

There are simply no more tears.

I continue to move through life numbly, void of feeling, as if I have somehow managed to turn my emotions off as simply as turning the knob on the faucet.

I work. I eat. I shower. I sleep. Repeat.

While I'm keenly aware that other people are having challenges and loss and devastation happening in their lives, it doesn't seem to lessen my pain to any degree.

I go to therapy. I sit on a white couch that once held both of us, and am told that I am putting my emotions in boxes. I rearrange the colorful pillows, uncertain about what to do with this information. This does not seem to help much.

I go on walks, only to find myself stuck in my head. Obsessing over the past. Details, memories, and images all play over and over, haunting me. There is a strange pleasure in the pain of reliving it all. Perhaps because then he is there with me, if only in my mind. This definitely isn't helping.

*I just need to keep breathing.*

I get together with friends, who support me in spite of myself during this challenging time. This helps as I know they love me, even when I have little to offer myself.

*Just breathe.*

Pain that had manifested in my body during the rocky ending has been turned up to a higher volume, reminding me I am going through an intense grieving process. The tension held in my jaw gives me radiating headaches. The knots in my shoulders and neck make it challenging to turn my head side-to-side. I have canker sores in my mouth that make it hard for me to speak or eat. It seems as though my heart could no longer hold the emotional pain, so it has overflowed into the greater being of my body.

*It's so hard to breathe.*

Rae suggests that I start getting bodywork. I feel a sense of relief that I am being given permission by her to do this, as it's not something I would allow myself to do. *Why is it that self-care fees like a luxury? Why is it that we are so hard on ourselves in the most challenging moments, when we actually need to be the softest, the gentlest, the most kind?*

In my first massage appointment, I become even more acutely aware of the tension that I've been holding. There is something inherently soothing about being touched. It's grounding. Healing. I can feel my body begin to let go. There are moments where I feel lighter, a sweet reprieve from the numbing pain I've been living with. On a deep level that I am only beginning to understand, there is symbiosis between my body, my heart and my mind. For this one hour each week, I know that I will reconnect with peace.

# WHAT NOW * RIHANNA

**B**its and pieces of peace begin to sprinkle increasingly into my day-to-day. It's been six months. I am feeling stronger, and decide to push myself to move out of Rae's house and into my own place. It's time to reclaim some of my independence. While I still have challenging moments, and I remind myself there will surely be more, I feel optimistic.

I find a place that feels good to me: the location, the layout of the space, the owner of the building, and the possibilities of being on my own.

Excited, I set up all the furniture in my new apartment, everything finding its place.

The fantasy of being on my own is quickly drowned by the reality of what I face being alone. Every time I come through the door, I am reminded that I am no longer with him. Each time I step in, my heart sinks. A broken record: I am alone. I am alone. I am alone. I sit on my couch after work, with minimal light, cold, feeling like a stranger in my own house. *I don't want to be here. Alone.*

Life, however, keeps on going. It keeps moving around me at the same pace it always does. It doesn't seem fair. But, that's how life always is for any hardship; it doesn't slow down for anything or anyone.

Little by little, I come out of my fog to notice the disparity between life's speed and my own slowness. Or, perhaps it's not the speed or lack thereof, but rather a disconnect. I realize that I need to reconnect, so I decide to go on walks around my neighborhood and notice what is around me.

I pay attention to the flowers I see. They are blooming, showing growth and beauty from the inside out, inspiring. The ones that really impress me are the ones coming up through cracks in the sidewalk. Resilient. Growing in spite of their circumstances. I begin to take photos to capture these moments of inspiration.

I come across an older couple holding hands, with a sparkle in their eyes when they look at each other. *Love can be amazing. What's their story?*

I look up at the clouds, amazed at how they are constantly changing, yet by definition and essence, they are always clouds. *I wonder if I can view emotions that way too. Always moving, changing, evolving. I don't like feeling stuck.*

I start to reconnect with myself. Haltingly at times, but reconnecting nonetheless.

I pick up a book to read.

I start to cook again.

When washing my face, I catch my own gaze in the mirror and smile softly at the eyes that look back at me, sad yet hopeful.

It is in these small moments I feel connected again.

I find myself most alive, however, when I am teaching. My dance fitness classes at the gym infuse vitality into my life. I choreograph a piece filled with kicks and punches to Christina Aguilera's "Fighter." It feels good to release some of the angry energy that's been trapped inside. Each time I move to it, I can tap into that part of my heart that is still tender and raw. *God, how long will it be this way?* I am being urged forward, encouraged by the momentum of life, movement, and connection.

# TRY * P!NK

*L*ife is passing by. I need to get back on the horse.

"I think I am ready to date," I share with Yesenia.

The conversation shifts to online dating, and our volume softens to hushed tones. When we notice this, we laugh about how funny it is that there's social stigma that warrants whispered voices in public when it comes to the topic. While I'd definitely prefer to date someone I meet through friends or in my everyday life, the reality is that with our busy lives, these days, most dating opportunities seem to happen through the Internet.

I join a free dating website. Uncertain I want to reveal myself completely, I decide to use a photo of a flower instead of one of me. *No one will probably click on me with this, but I'm not sure I want them to. If I see someone I'm interested in, then I can send him an email, sharing more details and a photo. It feels better to be under the radar and in control and to explore at my own pace and on my own terms.*

I send a message to a promising looking potential named Robert. We write back and forth several times before we proceed to chatting on the phone. We navigate the conversation successfully, making a solid connection, and both agree to a first date. *This isn't so bad! It feels good to be excited about someone. It's been awhile. I wonder if we'll like each other when we meet in person?*

Robert sends me a nice text saying he's excited to meet up. We end up texting back and forth about our days and how things are going until our date over the weekend. *It's so comforting to feel connected! And, perhaps distracted from the idea that I'll be single forever.*

Robert and I meet at a coffee shop. While I am nervous, he seems like a legitimately nice guy, and I also feel like I know him a bit from all of the texts from the past week. We chat about casual topics — living in the Bay, weather, the surface layer of our childhoods. When he asks if I'd like to go on a dinner date to get to know each other better, I wholeheartedly agree. *Can it be this easy?* We hug goodbye, and he says he'll be in touch about dinner. *Seriously, what a great start! Dating is really not that bad at all!*

Robert and I talk on the phone to coordinate the details of our second date. During the conversation, he requests a location close to BART. Out of curiosity, I ask whether or not he has a car. He informs me that he does, but prefers not to drive after dark due to questionable night vision. We finalize the details, wishing each other a good night.

The day of our date, Robert calls me from BART as I am looking for parking. I offer to pick him up since I am close by. (REARVIEW MIRROR: Agreeing to being the designated driver puts you at risk of being engaged longer than you'd like.)

As he gets in the passenger's seat, I smile, telling him, "It's nice to see you." After a quick, "Hi," in return, he immediately launches into how hungry he is. I casually inquire as to whether or not he had a snack before he came.

With eyebrows raised, he looks at me incredulously, throwing his hands into the air, and snorts as if I'd asked him something way too personal like, "Did you do your Kegels today?" He replies, "A snack? What in the world would I have eaten?" *Really?*

Being a huge advocate of snacks, I offer a few suggestions as I find an available parking spot on a side street. Upon hearing my recommendations, Robert replies, "Don't even get me started about how sick and tired I am of carrots." *Um, okay?* He continues, "Plus, I wanted to be sure to be hungry for dinner." *Fair enough.*

We get out of the car, and begin to make our way down the poorly-lit sidewalk. Robert missteps, teeters briefly, and nearly falls into the waist-high bushes before catching himself. I stifle my gasp, blurting out, "Are you okay?" He catches his balance and replies, slightly annoyed, "You could have told me the sidewalk was uneven." Attempting to hide my grimace, I smile at him, feeling slightly concerned.

The minute we are seated, Robert orders a glass of wine for himself. I place an order for red. The wine arrives, and before I have the chance to offer a toast, he begins to take big gulps of it as if he is drinking water after a hard workout. *Uh-oh.*

As we turn our attention to the menu, Robert cannot figure out what he wants to order. He moves the menu close to his face and then far away from him, squinting his eyes as if the lettering is too small or blurry. The waitress comes to check on us on several occasions. After the fourth time of checking to see if we are ready for food, he orders a second glass of wine. *Maybe he can't see the menu well since it's dimly lit in here?* I engage him in a conversation about what he has a craving for. Thin noodles or thick ones? Pesto or marinara? As he starts getting visibly flustered, I realize this isn't going to help the situation. He returns to staring at the menu with a perplexed expression. He says he is going to go for the spaghetti and meatballs. "Sounds like a great choice," I tell him. When the waitress reappears, he seems to have changed his mind at the last minute, and places an order for linguini and chicken.

After the order is placed, Robert takes another big gulp of wine and dives into a story about going to dinner with his ex and her family. *Oh, no! Is he really going to tell me a story about his ex-girlfriend right now?* Sure enough, he goes on to explain that during their college graduation dinner, his ex-girlfriend's father looked at the menu, and excitedly exclaimed "Oh! Look! You're on the menu! Black mussels." Robert proceeds to explain to me that just because he is a strong, black man, it was not funny to him.

As I acknowledge that it was, indeed, a very inappropriate comment, I mentally note that he <u>can</u> see the menu as he had seen the black mussels. He continues to tell me the full story about his ex-girlfriend, whom I notice he refers to in the present tense as "my girlfriend." *Argh. Doesn't he realize that talking about other women and exes on a second date is not good protocol?* I find myself sitting there, nodding out of politeness, with a deadpan expression on my face. He goes on to (over) share that, at the age of 44, he lives in a small studio and there has never been a "girl" he has ever considered living with. And then, somehow, I am listening to a story about how he was once in the hospital and he didn't even have any cute nurses to help him until one came in with a nice ass and thick thighs. *What? Oh my God! Can this be over soon? And, why am I still sitting here? I feel bombarded by his stories. What happened to the flow of conversation from our first date?*

While I have the fantasy of ending the date early, Robert orders a third glass of wine, consuming it at a slightly slower pace than the first two. As he takes another sip, I take advantage of the pause to shift his monologue from ex's and nice asses to work. As it turns out, he's rather unhappy with his current employment, and desperately wants to leave his job. *Why would you write on your profile that you enjoyed your job?* He's going to meet with his sister's friend, who is a career counselor, the very next day. Still attempting to make polite conversation and the best of the situation, I probe about what direction he is thinking of going, and he quips snidely, "How should I know? That's <u>her</u> job to figure it out." *What? Okay. I'm done.*

Yet, there is something inside of me that feels really bad for him. There will most definitely not be another date, but I am worried that he won't make it back safely to BART by himself with his vision issues. So, I decide to drive him. Pulling up to a temporary parking spot to drop him off, I immediately press the unlock button to open his door. *Almost there, Heather. Just a few more seconds.* Without taking the cue, he comes in for an awkward car hug. It feels especially so since I have no plans or desire to see him again. *Okay, bye-bye, Robert.*

He backs up slightly from me, and then swoops towards me, going in for a kiss. *Ahh!* I quickly turn my head to avoid it, barely dodging his lips on mine. *What is he thinking?*

As he realizes he has gotten the notorious post-date cheek swap, he belts out, "Oh! I see how it is! I go in for the kiss, and all I get is the cheek." I laugh-grunt a one-syllable "huh" sound as he quickly exits my car. *How could I have been so off on this guy from our first date? Is my intuition that off? Shit, do I even trust my intuition? Maybe I'm not ready for this dating thing after all. Let me try to stay positive.*

As I get ready to pull away from the curb, I take a big breath and congratulate myself on making it through my first official dinner date, noting that it turned out to be a strange experience. As I am taking another deep breath, I see Robert trip over the cement divider in the parking lot. He briefly teeters for the second time of the night, catches himself, and walks on without looking back. I shake my head at the evening of one-sided conversation involving ex's, nurse thighs, dodging unwanted kisses, and over the disappointment of something that initially felt promising.

That night, I receive a text that he made it home safely without falling into any more bushes. *At least he's got a sense of humor?*

The next day, I receive another text sharing, "You were right! Carrots and hummus are a great snack!"

Well-fed and without wine, Robert seems to be a different person. *Still. Not. Interested.*

I log into the website to send him a message. I thank him for the date and wish him the best in his dating search. I exhale and feel relieved as I press send.

What I do not expect, however, is an email back. He seems to be in total agreement with me that we are not well-suited for each other, but that I "seem nice enough."

I am not ready for such things in my life. I am not ready to sift through other people's shit. I am not ready to have to sit through bad conversations and feel the need to be polite, even though I know that's on me. I am just not ready. I delete my flower photo and close down my profile.

# I'M EVERY WOMAN * CHAKA KHAN

After telling Rae about my dating experience, I find my frustration and disappointment giving way to laughter as I relive the details. She sympathizes about it sounding ridiculous, gives me kudos for putting myself out there, and then tells me it's time to try something new. Not dating related, something just for fun. Her suggestion is a dance fitness class called "Shimmy Pop." We look up the studio, Hipline, and the website is adorned with pink, black, and gold, and screams "Sexy, Strong Female." *Not sure I'm feeling this.* However, I agree it'd be good to try to have some fun, plus we'll do it together, which always makes the unknown less intimidating.

In a room full of ladies, I find myself standing with Rae in the back row. Clad in black Adidas workout pants, a super baggy T-shirt, and a bandana on my head, I find myself shifting side to side, as if trying to get comfortable in the space and in my body. I notice ladies in class wearing revealing clothing. A few even have hip scarves that expose their midriffs. *I should have worn something different. Oh my God, Heather, you are fine. What in the world is your deal right now anyway? Why are you so nervous?* In the midst of critiquing my appearance, I realize the bigger issue is that I'm feeling insecure that I don't know what's about to happen. Even with a dance background, I can feel my insecurities bubbling up from deep within. *Will I be able to keep up? What if*

*I mess up? I hope I don't look like a spaz.* I smile uncertainly at Rae. She beams back. I try to ease up a bit. *Just breathe.* I look around the room again. There is such diversity of shapes, sizes, colors, expressions of uniqueness and beauty in this space. While a few other ladies appear slightly uncertain, most look at ease and comfortable in their own skin. *What's their secret?*

I feel butterflies in my belly as the teacher gives an introductory spiel about loving our bodies and having fun. As we start to move, I can't help but grin and then laugh outright at this instructor's outrageous comments. "Grab your butt, ladies! That's your butt! Look at it in the mirror. Love. Your. Butt." She is so entertaining that I step outside of my brain, my thoughts and my past. My body is not exactly able to do some of the movements she is asking of me. A shimmy that vibrates through my body, making everything jiggle? An undulating waterfall that starts with my chest and goes down to the ground? A side-to-side sway with the hips that not only pays attention to but accentuates my womanly curves? I feel uncertain. Yet, I don't seem to care. The teacher encourages and challenges us to go deeper. She encourages us to look at our eyes in the mirror, touch our bodies, find our own sexy, and fall in love with ourselves. It feels like magic. Without knowing exactly how, I sense that my life is about to change.

After taking classes for a couple of months, I am amazed by the expanded connection I feel with my body in these new movements while exploring sides of myself that are especially sassy and playful. My instructor finds ways to get us to tap into the many sides of ourselves, our 32 flavors, and reclaim the parts we want to bring more fully into our lives. It's about connection to self, to emotion, to womanhood, and to knowing that we are not alone in the often-crazy-ass journey that we call life. It's about embracing who we are wherever we are along our paths. In doing so, I start to feel and see myself. **As a strong, imperfect, crazy, beautiful, awkward, flawed, energetic, uncertain, hopeful woman.**

I work up the nerve to ask my instructor about the possibility of teaching for them. She smiles at me, saying, "That's so crazy! I was going to ask you today if you'd be willing to audition for us!" I am speechless. When I reply that I can teach a different class, without all the Belly Dance elements, her reply is, "This is what we teach here. You will learn it." *Really? I don't feel qualified. But, I really want this. It's become such a huge part of my life, something to look forward to.*

I begin teaching Shimmy Pop in the evenings and on the weekends, when I am not working with the kiddos at school or at the gym teaching my other fitness classes. While I feel uncertain about my ability to teach in this new style of movement, I also know this opportunity feels absolutely imperative to my healing process. I channel my emotions directly into my choreography. I put together playlists that feel like the stories of my life, which allow me to feel validated and connected. I find myself hollering to the ladies who take my classes, sharing insights based on my life experiences of heartbreak and healing, of working through insecurities to find strength, beauty, and uniqueness. Tapping into a voice that I didn't know existed. Finding a fierce side of myself that owns space like I never have before. I teach as if my life depends on it.

# AIN'T NO SUNSHINE * EMILY KING

As with most things in life, my path continues to be anything but straightforward.

I keep tabs on my Ex, compliments of Facebook. Mostly in the evenings. I can always tell when I am about to check on his status. I ask myself, "I wonder how he is doing?" followed with a brief contemplation of looking him up. Almost the moment my internal voice says "No, don't..." it is dismissed, and drowned out by my desire that is stronger. Similar to a child who, after hearing her mom say, "Do not eat some piece of who-knows-what" off the ground, promptly puts it into her mouth. Only I'm an adult, creating my own drama. In the very same moment I enter his name into the search box, I feel like shit about it. A Chex Mix of not-so-positive emotional ingredients. I just can't seem to help myself sometimes. I still miss him. I miss the life we had together. I don't want to. But, I do. *Still, why the fuck do I do this? It's self-inflicted torture. Do other people do this? Is it just me? Does he look me up too?*

I also spend time with a different ex-boyfriend who I feel safe to have comfort me. And though I have fleeting hopes he'll want to commit to me this time, I know he never will. While I don't want to admit it to myself, I know I'm filling the space. When we break up (again), I find myself in a heap on my kitchen floor. Crying for what could have been. For this hurt. For all my hurts. For what I want and do not have. I try to remind myself that these are all thoughts from past experiences that do not need to be my present. I attempt to assure myself that the discomfort is the thing that'll propel me to make change. It just hurts so bad in this moment. *Breathe.*

I find comfort in knowing that while my winding path is far from straight, it's moving, like the clouds I get lost in daily.

# KNOCKIN' * LEDISI

L ying out in Rae's backyard, enjoying the fresh spring sunshine, my phone rings. It's a blocked number. I pick up, thinking it must be my Dad, since he is one of the few blocked numbers that calls me. Instead, I am greeted by an extremely perky female voice. It's Amanda from a dating service.

Years ago, when I was in a more panicky state of finding "him," I'd called this professional matchmaking service. They took the process of selecting dates into their hands, giving it a "personalized touch." At that time, I decided not to pursue it due to the fact that "professional" translated into what I considered to be "very expensive," especially as a beginning teacher. For many months after my inquiry, the service would call leaving urgent sounding messages that included the acronym of their dating company and tell me, like they were my BFF, to be sure to call them back ASAP. *Seriously, WTF?*

Before I can barely say hello in return, Amanda excitedly asks me if I am still single. Due to my failed Internet disaster with Robert, the prospect of someone helping me with this dating process sounds appealing. *Maybe this is fate stepping in, urging me in a different direction? Okay, I'm going to be open to this.*

I explain that I've been single for the past year, and am ready to get back into the dating world. *Wait! Am I ready? I really <u>want</u> to be with someone, but am I actually <u>ready</u>? I don't need a man. I would just like one. Being alone is hard. I suppose it has some positives too, but I find it mostly hard. I'd prefer to be with someone. Yes, I really want to find him. I think I'm ready.*

My thoughts are interrupted by Amanda's sweet-as-maple-syrup voice, asking me, "How did you meet him?" in reference to my Ex. When I share we had met through a dating site, she uses it as a spring-board to inform me about how she is offering something different. I can hear the buzz words she has been trained to use: individualized approach, unique experience, success rate. *She's just doing her job, Heather. Stay open.* Amanda pauses, lowers her voice and stretches out her words, "Well, let's see. How old are you now?" There is a momentary pause as she seems to be looking through my records, before sharing with me, "Yes, well, this really is the time to find a real relationship before it's too late." *Too late?*

I take a deep breath. I calmly inform Amanda that I am not interested in talking any further. She asks why, so I tell her without any sugarcoating that using my age as a scare tactic as to why I should sign up with them is not a tactic or best practice for getting me to join. When she protests that she is trying to be helpful, I assure her that while it may not have been her intention to offend me, I'm no longer interested in using the dating service.

Proud of myself for standing my ground, I also can't help but wonder about the potential truth in Amanda's words. *I am getting older. Why haven't I found a lasting relationship yet? Well, I thought I had, but then it ended. It's taken me awhile to get through the heartbreak. It still hurts, actually. Am I through it enough to be open to what is next? I thought I'd be married with kids by now. God, I feel so far away from that reality. If I met someone, and we dated two years, how old would that make me if I were to have a child? Is it too late? Do I even want a kid? Shit, I can't go there right now. I just need to keep trying. Maybe I need to do something different. Am I not being open enough? Is it me? Why haven't I found him yet?*

# TRY AGAIN * AALIYAH

I'm informed by yet another person that she met her husband through an Internet site and they are happily in love. In fact, it was her <u>first</u> and <u>only</u> Internet date. *Oh my God! Really? I thought such things were up there with unicorn sightings, an urban myth, pure fantasy! But it's for real! Not a friend of a friend of a friend situation. It's <u>my</u> friend!* Based on her recommendation as well as my strong desire to find my partner, I join a different free dating site. This time, however, I remind myself that everyone on it is going through a similar process of putting themselves out there, so I upload a photo of myself. No flower.

As I am filling out my profile details, I receive a message from a man named Don. After a few back and forths, we make arrangements to meet for a glass of wine at a local bar the next evening at a local bar. *Okay, I can do this. Other folks really do meet this way, and there are happy endings that come out of it. It only takes one!*

Two hours prior to our date, I receive a text from Don, asking if it's alright to push back our meeting time to 7:35. *No problem, but it's a bit of an odd choice of time. Why not just round up?*

As I leave my house to meet him, it starts to rain, so I grab my umbrella before driving over. While looking for parking, which is unusually hard, I realize I am going to be a few minutes late. When I find a spot a few blocks away, I park and text him before I walk over, "Be there shortly due to parking."

When I arrive, I look around, but do not see him. I take a seat at the bar, and order myself a glass of wine. (REARVIEW MIRROR: Wait to order so that you are in the position to leave if your date is significantly late without a courtesy text.) The bartender makes small talk with me for a few minutes, and empathizes with the fact that I'm on a first date, but gives me further hope when he tells me he met his wife through a dating site. *Have faith, Heather. This can totally work.* After a few more minutes of sitting by myself waiting, an onslaught of different thoughts begins: *Will he show up? Will I recognize him? Wait, is that him? Nope. I feel awkward looking around. It's so obvious I am waiting for someone. Okay, I will just focus on my glass of wine. Let me not drink too fast, though. I should look around again. Where is he? What time is it?* I check my cellphone, which tells me it is now 7:45. I have no new texts. *Is he even coming? Oh wait, there he is!*

As Don walks towards me, barely making eye contact, he pulls up a barstool next to me, immediately flagging down the waiter, and orders himself a flight of wine. He proceeds to inform me that he is just coming from a hard workout, and loudly gulps down his glass of water. I have to wonder if the workout clothes he is wearing are the same ones he wore for his workout. Still without looking at me, Don shares that has not eaten that day. *Oh no! Here we go again. What is it with guys that are not taking care of their basic needs? And, he just ordered a flight of wine? I don't think I'll be able to last that long! I can tell that we don't have the right chemistry. But, maybe it's just a weird start? Let me try to stay open.*

As I take a sip of my glass of wine, Don dives into tell me his theory that we all end up dating the same person over and over again. He likes to look for the patterns. For example, he finds it interesting that he dates a lot of women who are very punctual, like me. *Hmmm. He is aware of his tardiness; he just doesn't care. He could have at least texted me.* When I comment that I appreciate when people are on time, he starts talking about time as a social construct. *Well, any which way, this is a definite no. I take a moment to revel in the punctuality of my clarity.*

I finish my glass of wine, half-listening to Don talk about the educational video work he does from home. I thank him for taking the time to meet up, and stand up to leave. He tells me that he is going to stay for another round before he walks home, if I want to join him. I decline. I also do not offer to give him a ride. *At least I've learned a few dating lessons - I do not have to stay out of a false sense of obligation or politeness, nor do I have to offer any rides.* Unfazed, Don stands up as well, excusing himself to the restroom, with a quick "Bye."

As I turn to leave, the bartender catches my eye, raises his eyebrow at me as if to say, "How did it go?" I give him a quick shake "no" with my head as I walk by. He nods his head knowingly. I shrug my shoulders and share a half-smile with him. *I wonder how many dates he has seen go down. I wonder how many more I'm gonna have to go on to find the right one. All I know is I'm glad that one's over!*

Trying to stay positive, I call Yesenia when I get home to give her the latest. We both agree that dating is not easy. The retelling of the play-by-play is entertaining, but getting out there and diving into these semi-blind dates is not. We are both intrigued at this notion of dating patterns. While I don't agree that we date the same person over and over, as Don asserted, it does give me pause to wonder about my dating patterns. *What sort of patterns emerge in my dating life?*

# LIONS, TIGERS & BEARS
## JAZMINE SULLIVAN

To explore my own dating patterns, I allow myself to go way back.

My first crush was in 4th grade. *Woah! That's really far back! Haha! That's where my brain wants to start though: my first remembered fire in the heart.* He wrote and performed his own plays for our class. Tall, striking blue eyes, super curly hair. He was magnetic. I was surprised that he liked me enough to give me a Valentine that simply said "from Drew," which I kept for years.

My first "official" boyfriend was in 8th grade. I thought he was super cute; complete with a striking tan, deep green eyes and feathered hair. *Feathered hair! The trends, I digress. Okay, get back to the focus, girl.* I was really nervous around him. I would go as far as to walk on the opposite side of the hallway when I saw him coming. The first and only time we kissed (just a peck) was at a party. I am pretty sure I ran away from him afterwards. *I was shy in general, but especially around boys. What was that about?*

The first guy I ever "kiss-kissed" was two years later. He was a crush, and I had not yet grown out of my shy shell. I was so nervous about whether or not I'd be any good at kissing. I also wondered why he would like me more than another girl in school who was way cooler and prettier. *Oh junior high. Such insecurities. Feeling like I'm not good enough does seem to be a pattern for me, though. And, while I feel like a confident woman, there are nooks and crannies that still hold that place of uncertainty. That's hard to admit as a 37-year-old woman; aren't I supposed to have things more figured out by now?*

My first relationship was in high school, with a badass biker. He sent me sweet handwritten notes in class for what seemed like an eternity (in actuality, more like two weeks) before we started dating. He's the one that turned me on to listening to a variety of music. He was also the person who inspired me to express myself creatively through clothing and poetry. He meant a lot to me, even though I knew at this young age that he was not my "one." Still, I wasn't able to cut ties when I went away to college, as he was a huge connection to my life thousands of miles away. It was also a time in my life that I was not at all skilled in communicating my needs. The imploding ending involved alcohol and different definitions of boundaries. *What a mess it was. What a mess I was.*

In hindsight, I met my first, true love when I was in elementary school, although we did not develop a romantic relationship until college. Because I had known him for so many of my formative years, trust with him was already established. He was the first man who wanted to know who I really was, asked me questions that got me to open up, and spoke directly to my soul. I remember standing in a doorway at his house, and he looked at me deeply, knowingly, and asked me what was in my heart. Around him, I felt happy and free and full and complete. We wrote countless letters back and forth for years, and got to know each other at a deep level. Years later, when we reconnected in person, the wildfire consumed us, like the stuff of fairytales. He was my everything. He had my heart completely. I would have done anything for him. When we were 23, our relationship ended. I wasn't sure

I'd survive without his love. We experienced a great loss and weren't able to make it through. He stopped showing up after that. Just kind of disappeared. I'm pretty certain he felt the same love for me, but it makes me wonder how he could have just walked away. *Feeling the love I felt for him and him choosing to leave seemed to also validate my underlying feeling that I did not deserve this type of love.* And, although many moons have passed between us, he still visits my dreams.

After the hard breaks with my high school boyfriend and then my First Love, I developed some hardness in my guarded heart. If a child touches the stove and learns that it is hot, she might try to test out the heat one more time, but she's going to learn pretty quickly to <u>not</u> touch it in order to not get burned. Isn't it the same for our hearts to a certain degree? It seems as adults, we keep trying to figure out how to touch without being burned.

When I began my teaching career post-college, I developed a long-distance relationship with a Grenadian architect who I met during my vacations there. He came to visit me once as well. A really solid person. Just not available for anything serious. Not sure if he will ever give up being a bachelor, as he seems to love his independence more than being in a relationship. I suppose for me, love was much easier and in some ways less complicated from a distance.

Then, there was a crazy-ass painter in San Francisco. Back and forth, up and down, every possible direction, for a couple of years. That was a doozy. While I think relationships require a lot of work, I do not think that they should be that hard. We remained "friends" for years on and off, which translated to getting back together once in a while, never amounting to anything positive. A charged relationship for sure. I would get voicemail messages from him, literally cursing me out for one reason or another. The complete opposite of what I grew up with. After a good therapist and a lot of work, it became clear that I needed to let go of any sort of relationship we had.

From one extreme to another, the next man in my life was a very sound, practical doctor. We saw each other for years running around the lake until finally, one rainy day, we stopped to chat. I really liked him. A lot. I found myself softening some of the hard shell, because of my desire to make our relationship work. Overall, things felt easy and natural between us. There was an inherent sense of trust that I felt with him. I found myself doing many little things to show him how much I cared — I cooked for him, picked up extra yogurt that I knew was his favorite, got him a "survival" kit for his car because of a conversation we had around a potential earthquake. I openly communicated and shared my strong feelings for him, something that I really worked. We spent two beautiful years together. Ultimately, he did not feel the same way I did, or it was too much for him. When he broke up with me for the second time in a Thai restaurant, he told me he was afraid because I looked at him with too much love in my eyes. *Too much love?* Any which way, he couldn't love me in a way that I needed and deserved to be loved. Another bachelor, perhaps for life. *I know I wanted more than he was able to offer, but it was good when we were together, and it was also a glimpse into what could have been. I guess "could have" is the operative phrase. It's strange when you "know" something is over, yet, a part of you still holds on. Is it brain versus heart?*

Enter online dating, round one. (This was when online dating was newer and the paid sites, in my opinion, were more reputable.) After a few unsuccessful dates, I ended up in a relationship with someone who looked really great on paper. On the surface, all was good between us. After getting to know him over time, however, it came out that he had issues with food and alcohol that he was not in a place to deal with. This started to affect our relationship.

Enter online dating, round two. After quite a few dates that proved unfruitful, I met and fell in love with my Ex, the only man I ever lived with. I wanted love so much, and when I met him, he was it. I could check off all the boxes of what I wanted. There was something special about him. About us. The only man I've ever yelled at. My beautiful relationship that ended in heartbreak.

*The men I've dated have been very different from each other. Perhaps it's that they have, in one way or another, not been emotionally available. Is that it? If I am the common denominator in all these relationships, what is it about me? I suppose approaching any new relationship from a hurt and guarded place could have something to do with it. But, aren't we all injured to a certain degree from past experiences? Plus, not trusting someone initially serves a purpose. There are some crazy folks out there, and it takes time to figure out who might be worth trusting. I mean, we all have a little crazy going on in one way or another. Don't we all have things we are working through? It's not like you have to have all your shit worked out in order to be ready to be with someone. I can think of plenty of couples that have individual and relationship issues, and they still make it work. I feel like I have done a lot of work on my own, and the next part is to do it with someone. I have to believe that with the right partnership, where there is a solid base of mutual respect, we will choose to work through life and grow together. Where is he?*

# BEST THING I NEVER HAD * BEYONCÉ

R eflecting on people significant in my past, I log onto Facebook. *Uh-oh.*

This time, I look up my high school boyfriend, the bad-ass biker, knowing that while I say that I don't want to know, I kinda-sorta also do. *Fuck.* Because I have blocked him in the past, I have to go into my settings to unblock him. *Clearly I've done this before, and I mentally blocked out that I blocked him. Why am I looking him up again? It's definitely not going to be helpful in any way, shape, or form.* Knowing it's not a good idea, I hit unblock anyway to take me to his page. *There's got to be an app out there for Internet searches that blocks all of your exes. I can't be the only one that looks up people from the past.*

There he is. Same profile photo as last time. No new information.

As I catch myself wondering again why I felt compelled to look, I press the button that gives me the option to block. However, I am met with a message in a box that informs me I cannot re-block him so soon; I need to wait for 48 hours before I can take this action. *What? SHIT! Now it's going to be in my mind, driving me crazy, for the next few days. Now, I can't let him go, because I have allowed that part of my brain to relive that shit. He is now taking up some of my mental and heart space. And,*

*I allowed it. I sought it out. I have to live with the decision I made that I know was not good for me. I'm so frustrated with myself. WHY?!*

After the deadline passes, I get back on Facebook to block him again. Another message in a box pops up, this time reading, "You've blocked X. We are sorry that you've had this experience."

*Indeed.*

# ONE IS THE MAGIC # * JILL SCOTT

Here I am. Well past what I thought would be my expiration date for finding love. I am still alive. I am still me. Even if I look up exes from time to time. Even though I don't cry much anymore. Even when I am sometimes challenged by being alone, without a romantic partner. Even as I give myself a hard time about being single or looking up exes. As Beyoncé sings, I am learning how to love myself, "flaws and all." In fact, I am rediscovering how to be on my own and actually trying to enjoy myself.

While I had previously noticed the gap between how I dance and teach — with freedom, happiness and confidence — and the everyday life I am living, I become even more keenly aware as the gap widens.

**I begin to consciously explore ways to live more fully, figuring out what brings me more joy.**

I buy myself flowers.

I get a pedicure.

I take time to paint and write.

I take myself out to eat.

While these things do not always come easily for me — especially dining out solo — I am determined to get comfortable with the idea that I can embrace being alone; that I'm worth being happy on my own. I want to enjoy my own company so that when he comes along, I will be ready this time. If I am not happy on my own, how can I be happy with someone else? *Wait! Is that what this is all about? "Him," someone I do not even know in the hypothetical future? Or me? I want to be happy. Period. Regardless of my status in a relationship or as a "single," I need to find my own damn happiness. Damn happiness? Haha! I am glad I can still make myself laugh as I'm getting all worked up. I'll chalk it up to owning all parts to myself.*

In my attempt to get more comfortable with my oneness, I walk into one of my neighborhood restaurants for dinner, to be greeted with the ever-so-popular question, "Just one?" I cringe slightly, as the question reinforces the singularity that I am facing, as well as the insecurity that I am trying to work through of being without an "other." I reply, "Yes, just me."

The next week, I am summoned for jury duty. Due to fact that we are not allowed to do anything other than sit in the "audience" while people get called into the juror's box, I tune in to the fact that one of the questions being asked of potential jurors is, "What is the present employment status of any person with whom you have a significant personal relationship?" *Well, how do you like that? There is not a prior question asking about whether or not people are even in a significant personal relationship to begin with.*

Intrigued, I start to observe people being questioned by the judge. Folks who have a partner answer, "My husband..." or "My wife..." In contrast, the people not in a "significant personal relationship" tend to look down at the ground, muttering something about "I'm single," or "I'm not in a relationship," or just plain old "No." *After all, we are supposed to paired up, right? But, what about those of us who are not in partnerships? Are we supposed to feel ashamed by our status? Especially as women, are we supposed to feel whole and complete only when we find our partner?*

As I am reflecting on this topic, I'm called up for questioning. When the judge asks me, "What is the present employment status of any person with whom you have a significant personal relationship?" I reply, "There is no status of any person with whom I have a significant personal relationship." Then, with an ever-so-slight-yet-undeniably-sassy head bob and deliberate pause between each word, I assert: "I. Am. Currently. Single." It gets a few giggles and smiles, and even the judge has a split second where his lip turned slightly upward before reassuming his poker face. I hope the point is also made that the question is presumptuous. I find that I am leading with my inner Shimmy Pop dance teacher persona more and more.

That night, when I go out to eat on my own, the waitress asks me, "Just one?" as she grabs a menu, looking around trying to figure out where to seat me. I take a breath, smile, and reply: "Yes, fabulously one." The waitress looks back at me, smiles knowingly and answers, "I heard that, love!"

I get a celebratory glass of bubbles to acknowledge the space I am claiming.

# FADING * RIHANNA

The following week, I meet Yesenia at one of my favorite restaurants to catch up on life.

After telling her my stories around jury duty and my single-gal eating adventure, we talk about the power of language, and how we are affected by it, whether we realize it or not. We decide the term "Wife Beater" tank tops should be renamed "Universals" since we both love to wear them for multiple occasions, but detest the name. We talk about how deeply gender differences play into education, womanhood, identity, and media. It also gives me room to pause to think about the references I make when I am teaching dance. I share with her that when I teach, I call my dancing ladies multiple things out of love: women, girls, warriors, loves, sweethearts, mamas, mamacitas. Or, how sometimes when I teach, I refer to "him" or "your man" and have been switching it to "partner" to be more inclusive and to deliver the message that the primary focus is about you and self-love.

From there, Yesenia and I somehow, and very ironically, find ourselves in the midst of typical topics for single gals: Why are there so many bad options to sift through? How do some women find what they are looking for so quickly, while we have not? What does it mean that we are still single in our late 30s? How can we be happy in so many areas of our lives and still want a relationship so much? What are we doing to make ourselves happy? Where is he? What do we do to find him? Why the hell is there so much focus on finding him, as if life is waiting to really begin until we do? How can we just live our lives, without attachment to our expectations or desires? What's wrong with wanting to find our life partners while still claiming our fierce and independent womanhood? How do we not let this take away from living our lives?

Yesenia and I simultaneously catch ourselves getting pulled down this rabbit hole and change the subject to our professional lives. She tells me about an upcoming interview she has the following week, which sounds promising. I pay for the bill as she tells me more details, mentally noting how nice it is to take turns getting the bill, with a natural ease.

Suddenly, in the midst of hearing about Yesenia's thoughts on her preparation for her interview, Yesenia looks directly into my eyes.

"Heather, I need you to keep looking at me."

"Um, okay," I reply hesitantly. While I trust Yesenia with my life, I cannot decipher the urgency in her tone.

"So, here's the deal," she proceeds, "Just keep looking at me. When I tell you that we are going to get up and walk out, I need you to follow me."

"Okay..."

"I'll explain later, just trust me," she assures me.

I keep looking at her. Then, she prompts me to get up and follow her. I am dying of curiosity. As we are about to walk out the door, I can't resist and look around, only to catch a glimpse of my Ex. With the one "friend" that I was slightly suspicious of throughout our relationship.

I can feel my heart beating faster. My breath more rapid. The world moves in slow motion as we exit the restaurant. *That was close.*

As we round the corner, Yesenia asks me if I'm okay.

"I'm not sure. That was just unexpected. Thank you for taking charge. I think I would have yelled at him if we had actually run into each other. How dare he be in my favorite restaurant! This is supposed to be MY restaurant. Not his! I introduced him to it on our first date. I should have the rights after we broke up." We both begin to laugh out loud at the ridiculousness of the last statements, even though there is a definite element of truth that dwells within it.

I drive home, wondering if it was coincidence. *I wonder if I will ever get to the point where I don't want to yell at him. That would be nice, as it doesn't feel good to hold onto that. It really messed up my life. It really messed up our lives. At least I don't feel depressed like I did before. I still feel sad about it all. And, a bit angry. I really don't like being angry. Maybe I need to figure out what lessons I learned from this. Let's see. I guess my path would be different; I would not have found Hipline, and would not be teaching Shimmy Pop if our relationship hadn't ended. Teaching has allowed me to reclaim, rediscover, and uncover new sides of myself, and I am so grateful for this work that has allowed me to grow so much. Can it be that simple, though? I mean, I wouldn't have chosen to end my relationship with him to find Hipline. But maybe life is like that in a peculiar way. We can't understand something horrible in the moment, but it leads us to where we are supposed to be. At least, that's what I hope to be true.*

# WHO YOU ARE * JESSIE J

Summertime rolls around, which I simply adore. It's also my birthday, which I celebrate with a trip. A lovely time with friends, I go to Mexico, trying not to focus on the looming number 38 and still being single. I focus on the good times and, the other parts of summer that I love so much: lying out in the sunshine, farmer's markets with juicy watermelon and heirloom tomatoes, longer days to cook and see friends.

After an especially amazing dance class, I walk through the natural foods store when I spot a man with the essence of a modern-day sexy saint coming towards me. Super tall, strong body, deep olive skin, long dreadlocks, direct eye contact, and undeniable confidence. We smile at each other as we pass. He appears to be too woo-woo for me, yet I am sparked by something about him. Straight chemistry sometimes just happens.

He approaches me in the next aisle, introduces himself as Raul, and shares that he is a martial artist and a massage teacher. He inhabits space more than most men I've encountered.

After chatting for a few minutes, he gives me his card, asking me to call him to set up an appointment. Naturally, I search for him online when I get home. While Google searches can pull up some info, Facebook gives a lot of information about people. To me, whether or not they chose to apply privacy settings says a lot in and of itself. So, I search for Raul, which is especially easy since his last name is also on the business card he gave me. I find pictures of him, full body painted in blue, dressed up like Krishna, wearing only a loin cloth. *How am I even considering him as an option? To each their own. This is not me. Yet, there is something there.*

I call Raul and we set up a date. And another. As I get to know him, I continue to be impressed by how he commands space. He does not seem to care about what other people think of him. As things progress, he stays over at my house. His body is unreal in terms of physical strength. Raul demonstrates a bridge position on my bedroom floor. Naked. It is impressive, yet I'm not sure what to make of such a prominent self-display.

He gets me to come out of some of my boxes. I walk around naked in front of him (no poses for me), let him hold me (it's been awhile), and get lost in kissing him. Opening myself to letting someone back in, I am reminded just how good it feels to be with someone. Even better, to have someone look into my eyes with great desire. Someone who shows up, and ultimately makes me show up in familiar and new ways. To reclaim desire. To reclaim my body in ways that are free and sexual and connected. *I really don't think he's the one, but maybe I'll just take on a summer lover. I've never been with someone with the sole purpose of having them as a lover. I'm 38. Why the fuck not?*

As things progress, I find myself in fascinating conversations with him around the topic of sex. Raul does not believe in fully coming. He believes, as some folks do, that when the male ejaculates, the energy or life-force is lost rather than being kept within the body. So, basically, sex is peachy keen by him, just not actually ejaculating. *What?!*

This goes against all of my previous experience, in which this seems to be the primary goal for men.

In a non-sexual way, Raul also talks about his work in massage, including what it means for him to hold space for people, to find blocks of energy and help find ways to release them. I am fascinated. He asks me if I've ever taken massage classes, as he feels that I touch in intuitive ways. While I dismiss this idea quickly, the seed is planted.

We both stop making an effort to hang out. A mutual fade. However, I begin to believe more deeply that people come (or not-come in this case) into our lives for more profound reasons than we realize when we first meet them.

# SOLDIER OF LOVE * SADE

I continue on with my daily life, mostly happy to be living more fully. Within a couple of months, I feel the urge to date again. Besides Raul, no one else has strolled into my life. I let my close friends and family know I am open to suggestions within their circles. One of my girlfriends has someone that she thinks would be great, so she investigates, only to find out he recently started dating someone he really likes, so he's no longer an option.

I work up the nerve to peek at a paid online dating service, as I am feeling more serious about dating this time around. I know people who have met through the free ones too, but can't help but think the paid ones might have more people who are looking for something more serious, since they are literally investing in the desired outcome. On the website, I see just enough potentials to pique my curiosity.

*I am ready! I can do this!* I psyche myself up and begin to enter my information.

First name. Last name. Email. Then, I am asked to choose a username. *HUH? I didn't think about this. I've been so focused on working myself up to this that the last thing I thought about was coming up with a username.*

*I don't know what name represents me. This seems really important, though. You know what, forget this. I will do it later.*

I give some thought to how I want to put myself out there in the online abyss. One of my favorite artists, Sade, pops into my mind as an inspiration. I put on a playlist that has mostly her songs, and when I hear "Soldier of Love," I know this is it. I have been through hardships in the name of this great thing we call love. I am still fighting for my heart, for the possibility of love within partnership to become real.

A week later, prepared with my username and a cup of tea in hand, I try again.

> Username:
> SoldierOfLove
>
> Tagline:
> The biggest thing in this world, bigger than the ocean and the sky, is your heart. ~ Do Hyun Choe
>
> Profile:
> I am grateful for so many things in life, especially the "little"' things — the perfect cup of black tea with sugar and cream, a flower blooming, making someone laugh, enjoying food with amazing flavors, massages, seeing a butterfly flutter by, lip gloss (just keeping it real!).
>
> I am also thankful for the "bigger" things — friends that are like family, after so many years, and figuring out my life path as a fitness instructor and literacy specialist.
>
> I am at a point in my life where I am happy with whom and what I surround myself with. I am thrilled

to have more time to do what I love. My social life is filled with friends. I am a fan of going out for a nice dinner or beverages. My favorite is bubbles, as I love to celebrate life : ) Because I am very active physically and give a lot in the work I do, I also enjoy downtime. Hot tubs are always nice. Going for walks and taking photos of flowers, clouds and urban art.

I am looking for someone who wants to be in a relationship. Obviously, dating has to happen as part of the process : ) but I have done enough dating in my life to know what I like and what I don't. I have a lot to offer and want the same from the person I am with. I want someone who wants to be in a relation-ship. For real. To laugh with. To talk with — deeply about life and also fluffier stuff. To cook with (or at least enjoy what I cook : )). To go for a walk with. To go out with, all dressed up. To stay in and chill some-times. To travel with. To be passionate with. To smile with. Someone who lives intentionally and also enjoys the finer things in life. Someone with heart. Someone who will be a gentleman in old-school ways and is also okay that I will open the car door for him sometimes too. Someone who has most parts of his life figured out and who also knows that it is a continual process to figure it out.

Someone who is looking for something special.

# DIDN'T CHA KNOW * ERYKAH BADU

**E**xcited, with a few butterflies in my belly, I begin searching. The first thing I pay attention to is the photo. To keep it real, there is sometimes an automatic "no way" solely based on the physical appearance that happens in the blink of an eye. There are some cray cray pictures out there! *It's kind of crazy how a decision is made so quickly. Why am I attracted to some people and not others based on a photo? How much of this is just superficial? How much of it is beyond that? What's involved in the split-second decision? What is it that makes an opinion form so quickly about a potential date being a viable option or not? I guess some men fall into the "maybe" category too, where I have to click to see more photos. For the most part, however, it's a definitive "yes" or "no" in a flash moment.*

That being said, an even bigger "hell no" comes from profile photos chosen deliberately in an effort to impress a potential match. I recognize that we all have different preferences and requirements in general, and I also acknowledge that plenty of men have perfectly fine pictures. The following profile photo findings are simply mind-boggling to me. **Guys**, if you happen to read this somehow, here are a few things to consider:

1. **Your profile picture should be of you.** Please choose a photo of only yourself in your profile picture. It is confusing when

there are multiple people. I went on a date with a guy with a profile photo of one guy who was pointing to another guy. I assumed he was the guy being pointed at. He was not. And since we are on the topic, while it's nice to see a pretty sunset or your dog, you can include those photos, but your profile picture needs to be just you. *However, looking back, I did put up that flower picture because I was not ready.*

2. **No matter how good you look in a picture, if you have to crop a woman out of it do not use this photo.** Yes, I can see her shoulder next to you and deduce that your arm is around her. Yes, I do see that wisp of long hair on your shirt. Yes, I understand that you did your best job cropping and there was no way to do a clean crop. No, I don't know if she is your relative, but it makes me wonder, and I have no way of knowing, so just don't.

3. **Please keep your shirt on.** OK, so this applies to even the most chiseled frame: You are reminding me of a nature special I once saw where the apes puff out their chests to show dominance. I know this may be a hard one to swallow, but really, it's great that you work out and take good care of yourself, but if you do have a "good" body, it will be a nice surprise. If we ever get to that point. Which we won't, if your shirt is off in your profile photo for the whole world to see. Note: the exception on this one is if you are somewhere tropical and the photo includes the surroundings. But, one is enough.

4. **Bathroom selfies are out.** Taking a photo of yourself in the bathroom mirror is a no-no in my book. While I get some insight into the cleanliness of your bathroom, I do not see the appeal of using it as your profile picture. Or, any photo for that matter.

5. **More than one photo, but less than twenty.** Please include more than one photo of yourself. Especially if it's blurry. Conversely, including more than 10-15 photos is probably more than enough. 34 is most definitely too much.

6. **Think about what you are portraying.** Watch out for that "I'm-so-sexy" look. You know the one, the over-performing come-hither one-eyebrow-slightly-raised other-eye-slightly-squinted. This is not a portfolio for being a porn star; it's a potential date and perhaps even a future spouse. Looking very serious, with no smile at all, or an expression that is frowning, scowling, or looks generally angry in any way, is simply not inviting. Especially if your tagline claims something like, "Fun guy looking for fun gal." Blowing smoke or appearing belligerently drunk are probably not the best looks. Unless, of course, this is a huge part of your lifestyle. In this case, thank you for showing me who you are from the beginning. Sharing a photo of a bath is one way to express visually that you are romantic. But, you are sharing it with everyone, which I do not find romantic. And, p.s., the fake candles are not really working for me. *I just can't.*

For any profile photo that speaks to me enough to make me curious to know more, I then move on to phase two of the screening process.

# WHAT'S MY NAME? * RIHANNA & DRAKE

A fter I see the profile photo, my eyes scan to the username. What does it portray? *Shoot, I wonder what guys think of mine? Soldier of Love. Does mine send any message that I am not aware of?* After spending time looking at many people, I can only conclude that some folks didn't take time to contemplate their username prior to entering their information. I have compiled a list of ones that made me roll my eyeballs, because even though I am very serious about this process, there has to be some laughter around wading through the sea, or perhaps Lake Merritt, of folks that are dating online.

BigSelfBaller
*Perhaps you are a self-made entrepreneur who is tall? Maybe you are talking about being an individual who likes to play with himself because of his larger size? Okay, that's kinda out there, but let's just say including the word "ball" in a username is probably not the best choice, due to the common reference of balls to cohones. In the context of a dating site, you may get some confused or disinterested ladies.*

MyLifeInPieces
*Are you going through a messy divorce and feeling like everything just fell apart? Do you compartmentalize your life so that each section is separate? Are you a fan of puzzles?*

WorkaholicSF
*Thanks for being so upfront about this. You are being very clear with where your priorities lie and I am going to simply say "Next."*

HardBankroll
*Perhaps cousins with Workaholic? Well, thanks for your honesty, but that seems like a pretty peacocky statement if you're trying to attract women based solely on your income.*

MrManIsMe
*Well toot toot for you! I am all about self-promotion and self-love. However, since I don't know you yet, I am uncertain if this claims confidence or screams conceited.*

MrRightNow
*Oh, hee hee! I think you may be my Prince Charming! KIDDING! Thanks for letting me know where you stand on the short- and (non-existent) long-term view. I actually applaud your honesty.*

Bring-on-2012
*Here here to the somewhat cheerleader-like enthusiasm! However, it's no longer 2012, and I am a bit wary due to the date disconnect. I know it can take some time to find the right person, but...*

SexyNSingle2013
*Sigh.*

Ganstahhh_Sinner
*Really? Come on, Oakland!*

Cutier_in_Real_Life
*Cutier? I know I like to make up words as evidenced by my spellcheck, but cutier?*

StankyDanky
*Ummm, what? Do you not smell good? Was this a cute pet name your mom gave you as a kiddo that stuck with you into adulthood?*

IThinkIMayBLost
*Best of luck finding yourself!*

Not_Very_Clever
*Sorry to hear, honey!*

MrScrewUSoGud
*Really?*

MajorStallionStudd
*Ai-ya! Did I really pay money to be a part of this site?*

Double_Stroke_Dude
*While I've been told that this is a drumming reference, it clearly makes me wonder about where your mind is. And your hand I can't see.*

IWearExtraLargeMagnums
*Way to put it out there?*

KeepItTightKeepItLose
*I think you mean "loose," but it really does not help the situation.*

## CarneConQueso

*Translation, "meat with cheese." Either you enjoy eating, or...*

## No1Special

*Ahh, come on now. Don't say you are No One Special. Or, wait do you mean Number One Special? Very different. Please watch out for names that can mean different things, especially when they are the polar opposite.*

## MrPeckerHead

*And, we have wiener. I mean, a winner.*

# NEVER GONNA GET IT * EN VOGUE

Looking at the profile photo and username happens in an instant. If these two pieces are in line, I'm going to check out the profile and channel my Nancy Drew skills. I'm going to read between the lines, so to speak, of what is being said to figure out whether or not I want to move forward to actual communication. Sometimes, however, no magnifying glass or lie detector kit is needed, as evidenced by the following:

- Looking for my soul mate. Haha! Just kidding!
- Hi. I'm a 39-year-old single man. Physically, I've got an average build but am in good shape. I've got black hair, and brown eyes. Some of my non-sexual interests include traveling, biking…
- I'm trapped in a glass case of emotions!!
- Yes, I'm intense and I ADORE this about myself. If you want someone much simpler to digest and swallow, there are plenty of fish out there who may better suit your wishes.
- I am cookie monster and I like all types of cookies.
- I'm indoorsy. I'm not the outdoorsy, camping, sports fanatic guy. I'd rather climb you than some dumb rock. (DIRECTLY FOLLOWED BY) Lots of chicks dig men who are not available.

I'm not one of those guys. I care more about what is between your ears than what is between your legs.

- I think that I need more friends in life, so I think I could say my life is lonely right now.
- I'm looking for a blend of happy, thoughtful, reflective, crazy, silly, loud, quiet, active, still and really soft lips.
- So what's the central tenant of my personality? I'm passionate! When I'm happy, I get excited like a 12-year-old. When I'm frustrated, trust me, you'll know that too. And when I'm trying to get stuff done, naked women dancing in my living room are unlikely to distract me.
- If you can make a girl laugh, you can make her do anything you want.
- My ideal first date has to be getting some ink done and then go home to lick each other's wounds.
- Top five things I can't live without: my Iphone, Netflix, my dog, my laptop and my dick.

*Really?*

Another component to the profile that I feel says a lot about folks is the age range they choose. At my current age, I set mine for 32-46, a relatively fair number of years in either direction. While I tend to date men who are a year or a few older than me, I am also open to dating someone younger. What does it say about you if you are 43 and the dating range, that you have chosen, is 30-36? You won't date someone within six years of your age? What about if you are 42 and the low end of your dating age range is 18. You are willing to date someone less than half your age? *Seriously? I know I have strong ideas about some things, but this just seems so crazy to me!*

Reading the profiles can be disheartening at times. The mild emotional sunburns I experience are inevitably a part of the online dating experience. Like sunburns, bad profiles are annoying, usually unexpected, and the reaction is REALLY? However, they seem to happen more often than one would think. AND, all this <u>before</u> you even go on an actual date! I suppose, bad profiles are somewhat entertaining. I remind myself to keep doing the doggy paddle through the water even if I'm too tired to do laps. *I just want one. The right one.*

# DÉJÀ VU * BEYONCÉ FEAT. JAY-Z

O n a daily basis, the dating site encourages me, via email reminders, to take action on the potential connections they send me. *Who has time for all this? It's like a part-time job, sifting through the site's idea of potential matches, which are sometimes way off, as well as all the people who have tried to make contact of one kind or another. I find it slightly uncomfortable to be in contact with so many strangers, some of whom I've run into in everyday life. Crazy! I remember Round 1 of online dating. I responded to every person who wrote to me, even if it was to say, "I wish you the best of luck on your search!" I got some rude emails back ("Who do you think you are saying 'no' without even meeting me? You should give me a try before you say 'no.' I could at least be a fuck buddy. And, the ones pleading that I give it chance. Too much. This time around, I'm just emailing back the folks that are possibilities.* I find myself mostly deleting these emails, and logging on only when I have a block of time and want to make it my focus.

I am flattered when I receive a special email informing me that I have been added to someone's "favorite" list. *He looks familiar.* When I open my account, I find that the man who has favorited me, Michael, is someone I dated in my second round of Internet dating. In fact, I remember going on a handful of dates, and really liking him until he just stopped showing up. *Hmm. What's he doing on here, favoriting me?*

*And, what's up with this feature anyway? What does this mean that I am one of your favorites?*

Upon reading his profile, it looks as though Michael has grown a lot since we last dated. He is no longer in advertising, and has changed career paths into the nonprofit world. He seems happier. He also has changed his original approach of looking for a "buddy to explore the Bay Area with" to actually wanting to settle down. Michael seems established and available.

*Is he just testing the waters by favoriting me?* I decide to "wink" at him to find out. The wink is a feature I prefer to favoriting. While it has the same cheese-level factor as sitting in a bar and someone literally winking at you, it shows direct interest to the person it is intended for. A virtual wink is a safe, efficient way to see if the other person is intrigued prior to proceeding forward with writing a longer message.

I am pleased to receive an email the next day informing me that I have a new message from Michael. *What will he have to say?* I open it. Informal chit-chat, "How are you? How is your week going?" Towards the end of his message, he includes the question, "Where did you grow up?" *Hmm, is he trying to verify it's me, or, does he really not remember who I am? That would be crazy, though. It wasn't just one date!*

I write back to him, answering his questions, including that I grew up on and off a military base in Spain. I also try as tactfully as possible to let him know that we dated a few years back, just by stating that fact. (REARVIEW MIRROR: If someone you dated doesn't remember you, walk away immediately at a very brisk pace.)

In return, he writes, "Hahaha! Why did you make me look silly? I did not recognize you because you look great, not so damn skinny as when we dated before." (Note: I am virtually the same weight as when we dated before.) At the close of his email, he includes his phone number, asking me to reach out to him.

Pushing back the bitter taste of denial, I am swayed by his cuteness as well as the memory of liking him, which does not happen too often. I call and leave him a message. *What the heck are you doing calling this guy that does not remember you? Are you really that desperate?*

The following day, he calls back and leaves me a voicemail. It contains some "interesting" clues, which I choose to ignore, or at least put on the back burner. ("Interesting" is the word that my therapist has pointed out I tend to use, usually not with positive connotations.) First he shares he'd been out drinking "way too much" for someone "his age." There are many audible sighs throughout the message. I do not go back to count them, but suffice to say, they are extremely noticeable. At the end, he informs me that I can either call him back that night or "whenever" later in the week. The lack of enthusiasm in his voice throughout the message is underwhelming. I take a pause on replying right away.

The next morning, I receive a text, asking if we can get together that night. I respond that I'm working until late, but we could chat via phone when I am done around 9 p.m. *Girl, you are choosing to be in contact with this guy.* I disregard my wiser self, who is telling me quite loudly this isn't going to work. My need for potential connection happens to be stronger than common sense at this particular moment.

When he calls that night, I pick up. We begin with small talk. A few minutes into our conversation, Michael brings up not recognizing me. I share that I was surprised that he didn't recall me, because we had gone on a good handful of dates. In fact, we'd kissed. He immediately follows up that I should "not hold it against him." *Hmmm. I thought we'd had chemistry that does not come along every day.*

As the conversation closes, Michael half-heartedly says we should get coffee or "something," which we both know we won't. *I'm not sure what I was hoping for, but how was I even considering going out with someone that didn't even remember kissing me. Sometimes I feel like I am being too harsh, and other times like I'm not harsh enough. This guy literally forgot me. That's absurd.*

# BRUISED BUT NOT BROKEN * JOSS STONE

I feel determined not to be discouraged by this particular ghost from my past who ended up making me feel forgettable. I try to let go of the bitter taste upon receiving a few more emails which appear to be very suspiciously cut and pasted (most likely to multiple women). Even though I've had zero actual recent dates, I feel the need to try again.

I find a nice introductory email from Jonathan. I write back, sending my phone number immediately, as I do not want a repeat of building up a virtual relationship like I did early on with Robert. After briefly chatting on the phone, Jonathan and I make arrangements for a first date later in the week. He suggests meeting at a small jazz bar. *Promising*!

We meet up. He is cute. Slightly nerdy, which I find endearing. We have an upbeat conversation. His quirky cuteness reminds me of my ex-boyfriend, the doctor. (REARVIEW MIRROR: If someone reminds you of an ex from your past and you can't stop making the comparison, it's probably not going to work.)

Before the date ends, Jonathan arranges for a second date early the next week. *Yay for plans in advance!* He says he will be in touch to firm up the details. I mark my calendar, already looking forward to seeing him again.

The day before, I realize that I haven't heard from him, so I send a text to figure out where we should meet. I do not hear back. *Hmmm.*

There is no word from him the following day either. *Shoot! I thought we had a really sweet connection. Well, I guess it's better to know earlier rather than later.* Yet, I can't help but feel disappointed.

Attempting to lift my spirits, I call Rae, who sympathizes with the fact that I didn't hear back from this guy, and she invites me over to watch a movie with her and her husband. *Navigating these choppy dating waters can be daunting. From last minute invites to emergency debriefings on this adventure, I am so grateful for my friends.*

Fifteen minutes prior to when Jonathan and I had originally planned to meet, I receive a text informing me that he is running late, asking me where I want to meet up. *Huh?*

I text him back, letting him know I made other plans, as I had not heard back from him. He responds, "My bad. I forgot to look at my calendar, and didn't see your text until now. Maybe some other time then?" *Oof. Not only did he forget, but he also tried to play it off like he didn't. Let me try not to take it personally.* I text back wishing him well on his dating search. *Should I have cut him more slack? Maybe I am just feeling bitter because Michael forgot who I was right before I made plans with Jonathan. But, no. Geez, is it really that hard? I want to be with someone who is excited to see me. I realize that there are hella options with online dating, but I want someone who doesn't forget about spending time with me. Who wants to spend time with me! I'm pretty sure that really isn't too much to ask for.*

# LOVE ME UNIQUE * MICHAEL FRANTI

I fall asleep and dream of "the one," lying next to me. I do not see what he looks like, because my eyes are closed in my dream as well. But, I sense him. He is there. The feeling behind us together is beautiful. Unique. Heartwarming. Assuring.

When I wake, I feel comforted. I am completely at ease. I have a deep knowing that the timing has simply been off for him or me so far, that we've had to learn certain things before our paths come together for us to finally meet. *I know this sounds kind of unreal, but I felt him. He's out there, and we're getting closer. We both need to be on the same page at the same time. I need to maintain my faith in love.*

# VA VA VOOM * NICKI MINAJ

Inspired by my dream, I remind myself to keep on keepin' on! I turn to online dating yet again, as I am unsure how else to channel this desire into action and reality. *As a grown woman who is working a ton and does not go out clubbing or to bars, where else would I meet men?*

I write back and forth a few times with Joe before we set up a first date. I know from his profile that he is very tall. In preparation, I put on my highest wedge platform shoes (lending me an extra four inches), and my bangs are poofed up in front (adding another one and a half inches). I am still way shorter than him, and what 6'7" sounds like and looks like are definitely different, especially when waged against my natural 5'5" sans extra assistance.

When we arrive at the bar, Joe is super friendly to me. And to the waiter. And to the other waiter. It's almost like he's a celebrity. *Perhaps he was in a fraternity?* Once we are seated at the bar, I notice him referring to everyone as "friend." Let's call our "friend" the bartender over. I am not sure that our "friend" the waitress saw us sit down because it's so busy. Taking note of his super-friendly nature, we settle in for a drink.

Since we were seated at the bar, we are physically close. Joe pats my hand. Then my shoulder. Then my leg, at which point I move slightly away from him. (REARVIEW MIRROR: If your date attempts some flirtatious touching, and you are not feeling it, the chemistry and vibe are most likely not there.)

I also tune into the fact that Joe winks. A lot. Don't get me wrong, I like to wink too. In fact, I encourage my dance ladies to wink at themselves in class on a regular basis. However, being on the receiving side of about 11-ish winks within a one hour date is simply too much for me, especially when it's with a lingering wink, attached to a comment like, "Oh, girl, I have a really good feeling about us. I mean, I know we just met, but this connection I feel is too good for it to mean nothing. You feel me?" *It feels ridiculous that I am annoyed, but I am. I shouldn't be annoyed on a first date. It reminds me of that special I watched on Discovery last week about all the pieces that come into play when two potential mates meet. What was it called, "The Science of Sex Appeal"? We don't even realize all the things going on that make us attracted to someone— the scent of the person, dilation of the pupils, tone of voice. Although it didn't talk about winking per se, I do know that my chemistry is off with Joe. I am finding small things annoying. Is that valid or is it just me? Shit. Well, any which way, it is what it is. It's a no.*

# ME, MYSELF AND I * BEYONCÉ

I log back into my account when I get home to try to assuage my current state of vulnerability over another no-go, and to try to prove to myself that I'm not <u>too</u> picky and I'm doing my best to stay open. I find three new messages.

One message is from a man who had invited me out for a glass of champagne three days prior. *That sounds nice. He clearly read my profile to know that about me!* Then, I see a second message the next day that simply reads "?" as if he is waiting for my reply. Then, I see the final message sent a bit later that same day that reads "..." as if he was still waiting for me to answer him and I left him hanging. What is so strange, is that he can see that I haven't even been on the site to answer him. *So impatient!* I get it if I had been online and didn't reply, but I clearly have not been. *What's this feature of being able to see the last time your potential person of interest was active on the website about anyway?*

Another email is from a guy who asks me three questions a) How physically affectionate are you? b) What are your thoughts on public displays of affection, and c) What are you views on premarital sex? I shake my head, fluttering my lips as I exhale, and close the email. *Bye-bye!*

Lastly, there is a message from a man who comments on one of my photos, "You sure are super sexy here! What a smile! I hope you don't mind my commentary, but your sexiness deserves to be worshipped, and that's what I'd do for you, given the chance. Let's make it golden! What do you say, Sexy?"

*Geez, there are some interesting folks on here. Even though the chemistry wasn't working for me, at least Joe seemed like a nice guy. For now, I think I need to take a dating break yet again, and come back to myself. This is too much.*

# FEELING GOOD * NINA SIMONE

While my thoughts and experiences with dating and chemistry are muddled, I feel fortunate to receive weekly massages that act as a source of peace through it all. While it's beyond words to try to describe, I can tell that the consistent process of receiving bodywork is shifting things deeply within me. My body and heart are balancing, softening, opening.

At the end of one of my sessions, I ask my massage therapist what led him to do bodywork. He shares it was something that he was drawn to, without thinking too much about it. My curiosity becomes sparked when he mentions that a colleague he respects tremendously is attending school right here, in Oakland. *While I realize that giving massage will be different than receiving, I know how deep and profound bodywork can be, and I feel that I would like to share this with others. I need to move toward this excitement!* I make the decision right then and there to look into it. I feel grateful to life for placing my next step in front of me in such a straightforward, knowing way. I also give a mental shout-out to my summer lover, Raul. *I never expected this to be my path, but here I go!*

I tour the local massage school. While it makes more sense for me to study Swedish and Sports Massage with the work I do in the fitness world, I feel myself drawn to the theory and practice of Shiatsu. When the teacher brings us into the upstairs room that is lined with a series of small, open windows and a wind chime gently sounding, I feel immediately at home in the space. When he speaks from his heart about his insights into Shiatsu, I feel as though I could listen to his wisdom for years.

The approach of Shiatsu is based in Chinese medicine, which is very different than how I was brought up to think about health and the body. What resonates most with me is the idea that the body and heart are constantly trying to find balance as they are thrown off by both external and internal factors. *Ain't that the truth? For me, this also includes external and internal factors of modern-day dating: bad dates, judgment, self-judgment about the judgment, feeling hopeful only to have something not work out and, ultimately, still being alone. Sometimes, I feel like the strong Soldier of Love that I present myself to be, and other times a vulnerable girl whose heart has been broken and who just wants to be loved. Dealing with all these factors, what I realize is that rather than having the expectation that I'll always be in balance, the focus is on how to keep coming back to my balance when I'm thrown off.*

In the beginning, when I practice massage, I mostly feel awkward. I find myself holding my breath, tightening my jaw, and storing tension in my shoulders as I try the techniques I am being taught. I am confused and somewhat overwhelmed by the amount of information on deeper theory and rich history that flow over me in waves. I also battle the voice in my head that says I am not good enough and that I am doing it all wrong. My teachers are so calm, so centered, so sure that everything will be okay.

I am lucky to have friends who let me practice on them. And, somehow, in spite of myself, I find moments of turning the thoughts in my mind off and simply doing what feels right. I also get positive feedback. *If other people trust me and think I am good enough to come back to for sessions, I must be doing something right.* These moments string to-gether and allow me to realize that this form of bodywork, and help-ing others, is part of my path. Not just my career path, but similar to teaching dance, for my own heart's healing.

# NO, NO, NO PART 2
## DESTINY'S CHILD FEAT. WYCLEF JEAN

Optimistic about the changes happening in my life, I decide to approach online dating again. It has become clear that it happens in phases. Stop, go, stop, go. It's as though after each experience, I need to take a break and find my way back to my center in order to stay grounded, happy, and ready to put myself out there again.

This time, I jump back on the site, feeling determined. Up pops Chuck. I read his profile. Upon seeing that I have viewed him, he shares a wink with me. After reviewing his profile, I wink back. From there, he emails me and I email in return, including my phone number.

I receive my first text message from Chuck the next morning that he had sent the night before. At 12:37 a.m. It states: "It's Chuck from the dating site. How you doin'?"

Sigh.

It's late at night. You don't know me or my lifestyle or what time I venture into la-la-land. It never looks good when you are texting that late at night as it can very easily be perceived as a booty call. While I'm not on the I'm-waiting-till-we're-married sex plan (although it's been awhile!), you are definitely going to have to show me a lot more than putting up your tail feathers so early on. Seriously. Not interested. Or, perhaps that's not what you intended at all, and it's a sign of not being mindful of time and boundaries. I don't know what else to think. *Not even my best friends or clients text me this late at night.*

In addition, while I totally get that we are in a world of modern-day technology where text messaging is the acceptable means of correspondence, it's also okay to call with a real "hello." Go ahead, hon, pick up the phone. Let's have a conversation. Really, I already gave you my number. It's safe to call. *I am sure it must be challenging to navigate dating from the other side as well. Am I being too hard on him?*

The next morning, I receive an email message via the site from Chuck. It reads: "Hey! Was wondering if you didn't get my text message or if you are just blowing me off?" *Hmm. Red flag?* I look at his profile again, and he seems to be a professional man, looking for something serious. *There aren't that many men out there that I'm interested in getting to know better. Give him a chance, Heather.* I write back, "Hi there, Chuck! If you would like to talk, please feel free to give me a call."

Later that day, I receive a voicemail from Chuck:

Helloooooo, Heather!! This is Chuck, journeyoflife, from the dating site. How YOU DOIN'?? So, I'm calling you because CLEAAARRRLY texting was (pregnant pause) SO WELL received. Arrr, Arr, Arr. ANYways! Ummm. Sorry I missed you. Mmm. Home from work, doing laundry, trying to procrastinate about what I'm going to eat for dinner because I'm SO NOT FEELING trying to figure out what I'm going to do. AN-Y-wayzzz, umm, such is life...until I get a maid. Or, a cook I guess, duh, because I ALREADY have THE MAID. But, anywayzz, call me. Would LOVE to talk to you. I can be reached at this number. And, ummm, talk to you soon. Hope this finds you well. Ummm, Bye.

*Woah.*

Later that day, before I have a chance to call him back, I receive VM #2. This one is with a lot of background noise from driving on the freeway while calling:

HEATHER! IT'S CHUCK, JOURNEYOFLIFE FROM THE Internet. Alright. Trying you aaaaagain. Come on, girlfriend...NO ONE IS MORE APATHETIC ABOUT THIS ONLINE DATING THING THAN ME, so don't be trying to go and take my title, OKAYYY?!! So, CALL ME. (Laughter) Talk to you later. OH, and I hope this finds you well.

At this point, I can't help but start laughing out loud. *Who is this guy?* I check in with myself to see if I am feeling apathetic: nope. I reread my profile to see what kinds of messages I may be putting out there, to be sure I am not putting out the vibe of something like apathy towards dating: negative. A bit judgmental in my thoughts: yes. I remember that Chuck is divorced, a bit older, and I conclude maybe, just maybe, he is really clueless and reaaaalllly nervous about dating. *Maybe?*

So, we talk on the phone. After a few minutes of chatting, he asks if I want to meet Saturday mid-morning. My mind is telling me "No!" but my mouth is somehow verbalizing "okay." *Why did I just say yes? I really need to work on the art of saying no in the moment.* As we are getting off the phone, he utters a muffled comment that involves the word "sexy," to which I say, "What did you just say?" Chuck follows up with a quick, "Oh, don't worry about it at all. Just pretend I didn't say that. You didn't hear anything." *Umm, what?* (REARVIEW MIRROR: I'll let you fill this one in!)

Baffled, we hang up, and I put in my mental Rolodex to text him to cancel our date the next day. However, before I have the chance to do so, my phone vibrates. A text message from Chuck reads:

> Hey Heather! So, I am not feeling that excited about meeting with you tomorrow. I told you I'm pretty apathetic about this whole damn online thing. I'm thinking I need to just cancel on you. What are your feelings/ thoughts on that?

*My feelings and thoughts? This guy is too much! We've never even met. And, now, he's cancelling? Which is fine, but he does* <u>not</u> *need to know my feelings and thoughts on this. He cancelled. End of story.* I do not reply.

On Saturday, I drive down to Pacifica to visit my childhood friend, Chantal, and be by the ocean. I turn off my cellphone when I arrive and enjoy the day with her. We catch up on life, and have an amazing conversation around what I am learning in Shiatsu, as she is an acupuncturist, and uses the same methodology I am learning about.

Before heading back to Oakland, I turn my phone back on. I am puzzled to see a message from Chuck. It reads:

> I am assuming you got my message??? I came to the coffee shop just in case :-)

*What the heck is going on with this guy? Mr. Self-titled Apathetic showed up for the date he cancelled and is leaving me a smiley face?*

Bye, bye, Chuck. I am not eligible to be your new maid or your "sexy" something. *Sometimes you gotta say or sing, "No, No, No!" for the "Yes!" to come.*

# THERE YOU GO * P!NK

I don't take too much time to reflect or pause on this one, as it was so outrageous it doesn't seem to warrant too much reflection. I get back online and find Henry. He has super cute photos and I'm drawn to the openness and humor in his profile. He is an acupuncturist, which I find especially appealing.

A few days after sending him my number, I receive a late-night text that reads, "U up Henry." Between the misspelling, poor grammar, lack of tone, and the time he sent it, I must conclude that texting may be the worst thing that has happened to dating.

The day after the text, he also calls. *Yes!* I pick up the phone, and thoroughly enjoy my conversation with Henry. He's quite funny in real life as well!

He sets up our date to get cheesecake in Walnut Creek, which I think is a really cute first date idea. When we meet, I find him to be a bit "Rico Suave" for my taste (e.g. shirt undone at the top with some chest hair blowing in the breeze, some kind of big necklace and smelling of cologne in a slightly overpowering manner). Catching myself in judgment, I take a breath and focus on showing up. The date itself is very fun. I do notice that he talks pretty much nonstop for the majority of it, but in a very entertaining fashion.

As we leave the restaurant, it begins to rain, so we say our good-byes quickly and I head back to Oakland.

I receive a text from Henry the next day, informing me that he decided to "break the wait 3 days to call rule." I playfully point out that the rule applies to actually calling, and I'm not sure it applies to texting. Henry texts back with a smiley face, saying he is happy that I am already "calling him out," and lets me know that he will call me the next day. Which he does. *Fantastic!*

The conversation has a nice flow. We laugh a lot, chat about random things, ask a few more questions about each other: all standard in the getting-to-know-each-other process.

Towards the end of the conversation, Henry announces that he would really like to ask me out on an "authentic" date, but he does not feel he knows me well enough to do so. *Wait! What?* If I am "open" to it, he'd like to meet on Saturday night to "hang out" so perhaps at the end of it, if all goes well, he could get to the point of wanting to ask me out "authentically." *I'm so confused! Didn't we already have a date for cheesecake? If that wasn't a date, what would you call it?* While I am struck at the oddity of this approach, we set another "non-date" at a prime date time: Saturday night at 8 p.m. (REARVIEW MIRROR: If you are confused by different definitions of what constitutes a date, it's probably not going to work out. However, it's also better to clarify things at that moment than wait to see how things play out.)

The next day, I receive a text photo from Henry. No title or comments. Just a photo. It has no bearing on our conversation from our first non-date date at all. No reference can be taken from it, no parallel can be drawn. Nada. Not a thing. Zilch. The photo is a middle aged man with long curly hair, balding in the front, sitting on his carpeted floor. The man has an electric guitar in the background and a myriad of guns laying around him. He is wearing speedos and sitting with his legs wide open. *Well, my Saturday night just opened up.*

Before I've made up my mind about how I want to respond, I receive a succession of three texts from Henry, spaced about ten minutes apart.

Text one: How did this tickle your fun-oh-meter?

Text two: Crack a smile? Or, an outright, out-loud abdominal workout you laughed so hard?

Text three: Or was your reaction, what kind of douche would send me this picture?

I sit and take a deep breath. *Really?* I reply, "I find it entertaining and bit disconcerting that you do not feel that you know me well enough to ask me out on a proper date, yet you think it is alright to send me an inappropriate photo that has no relevance to anything."

Henry texts back, "It was a joke! I thought it was hilarious." I decide not to reply.

A few days later, I get a text from Henry with an invitation to a party, "FYI, there's a great singles event coming up. We are getting a limo so no driving issues. UR welcome to come as a friend."

From here, I decide to investigate how to install the blocking feature on my phone. While chatting with the technician, she inquires about the phone my child has. *Huh?* After realizing her confusion, I explain to her, "I don't have any children. I need to be able to block numbers for my dating life!" She laughs as she explains that the blocking feature is listed under "Parental Control." We both joke that it is needed for much more than that! For a few extra dollars a month, I am able to block the numbers of unwanted dates. (Note: Thankfully, paying for blocking is no longer required.) Being able to block someone makes me feel like Wonder Woman with her private jet: I can disappear when needed.

# PRIVATE PARTY * INDIA.ARIE

In contrast to my dating life, my non-dating life continues to cruise along smoothly. I deepen my massage practice work by taking Advanced Shiatsu. Teaching my dance fitness classes, I am ecstatic about the levels of connection, emotion, and release. I am enjoying and appreciating my friendships wholeheartedly. I am in love with life. I recognize that I work a lot, but I know it's a part of developing a business. It's a lot, but doable. It's dating that I find to be exhausting.

When the opportunity presents itself to leave the city, I opt for the dating breather. My friend Anna invites me to spend the night at a clothing optional spa. While my initial inclination is to say no, I remind myself how refreshing it is to take some time away. Plus, sometimes my life gets a bit too routine. I tend to go to the same restaurants and order the same favorites. I do this because I know I love it and I won't be disappointed, but it also means I won't find new favorites. I can't help but wonder if I have become more this way in the bigger picture of my life. Thus, in my Let-Me-Be-More-Open mentality, I agree to go. *Who am I to never have had a naked experience in public anyway?*

We arrive at night and head to the hot tub. This is a great way to start, as it's dark and I can't see much. I get to ease myself into the whole idea that it will not just be me that is naked. I actually enjoy lying out naked to get sun by myself. I also have been to a women's day spa where we were naked. There's absolutely nothing wrong with being in our natural bodies, it's just new to me in a public arena, especially with men. *Maybe it will be similar to the ladies spa?*

Anna has forewarned me that I might be asked by a massage student if I want a Watsu, a water massage. She explains that a friend of hers usually gets them, and for the most part, they have all been innocent, except for the time that she had a cupping of her butt cheek. *Hell no.*

Sure enough, while in the hot tub trying to mentally let go and embrace my inner woo-woo-ness, I am approached by a man offering me a Watsu. I look at him with mild alarm and in a shout whisper reply, "No thank you!" While I love massage, the story involving butt cheek cupping by a naked stranger is at the forefront of my mind.

Some time passes and I find myself having a hard time being still. I hold on to the edge of the pool and start doing gentle froggy kicks behind me. I am enjoying the way the water feels and start to think about how much I love being in water — it's relaxing and feels very healing. Then, I am shocked to find that I have just swiftly kicked Watsu man in the butt as he's whisking another woman around the pool.

I stop my kicking. *I need to embrace my inner and outer stillness.*

After our hot tub adventure, we end up sleeping outside under a gazillion stars. It's so beautiful.

In the morning, when Anna and I are finished eating breakfast, I notice there are a ton of people lying out in the main area. I have never seen so many different sizes, shapes, colors and varying degrees of hairiness in my life. *Just making an observation.* I decide that I am going to make my way to the top deck, where there is only one man sleeping and one woman doing naked yoga. *This isn't so bad. I definitely like having my personal space.*

Anna comes to find me a couple hours later, and we head to the main pool for a dip to cool off. I feel my judgment skyrocketing. *Uh-oh. I'm trying to be less judgmental in life, but this is slightly ridiculous to me.* There are people there clearly just enjoying being in the sun. There are other people who are there clearly to flaunt their nudity. Striking poses as if they are Greek statues. Framing their Goodies with their legs at certain angles. Like all they need are some grapes and a glass of wine in order to have someone paint a portrait of their exquisiteness. I decide to leave the scene, and go back to my safe haven on the upper dick. I mean deck.

After another hour of soaking up Vitamin D, it is time for me to pack up. It has literally been an eye-opening (but pretending-not-to-be-looking) experience. I am ready to go. As Anna walks me to my car, we joke about how "my man" is most likely not going to be found here.

Then. There he is. Naked man. On the front lawn. Hula hooping. *Goodies in a rhythmic swirl. It's time to go.*

Beautiful things can come out of new adventures. Like seeing the stars and getting perspective that you wouldn't get otherwise. Like sharing an experience that you can laugh about for a long time afterwards. Like pushing your boundaries to find what lies beneath. It's about the balance of begin open to the new, while also remaining grounded and true in knowing what you like and don't care for.

# SAVE ME * NICKI MINAJ

Back from my adventure, I take another stab at dating. I set up dinner with a guy who happens to be my height. I would usually disqualify him, but I realize that if he has all the qualities I am looking for in a partner, then his height shouldn't be the deterrent. *I must admit I really like the way bodies fit together with men who are taller than me, BUT height should not rule someone out automatically. It goes back to that being open while knowing what you like.*

I agree to meet Ram for dinner, going against my general rule of drinks only. Because he is making an hour drive for our get together, I feel my "yes" to his suggestion is warranted. (REARVIEW MIRROR: No dinner dates when meeting for the first time. No. Matter. What.) From the moment we meet, however, it appears to me that Ram is not comfortable. He walks in a very stiff, staccato fashion as if his shoulders can't move because he is puffing his chest up to be bigger than it is. *Am I projecting this onto him?*

We walk to the bar, and Ram flags down the bartender with a hand gesture and a slight scowl on his face. *Try to stay open, Heather.* When the drinks arrive, I thank him for driving all the way up to meet. "No big deal," he replies. When we are told our table is ready, Ram grabs my drink out of my hand, so that he can carry them to the dinner table. *No, I'm pretty sure he's not comfortable. I also don't know about this dynamic between us. While I can appreciate when a man takes the lead on ordering drinks and offering to help carry them, what is coming across seems like a need for control.*

We are seated outside by the beautiful waterfront view, and Ram launches into a saga about his low-carb diet as he peruses the menu. He is working with a nutritionist, and shares with me that most of his meals are protein drinks and supplement bars. *Yikes! Is this supposed to impress me? Maybe he thinks it will since I'm in the fitness world? Or, maybe he's just really proud of it for himself.* We get into a brief conversation about this, and I share with him that I'm an advocate for food straight from the source as much as possible, and listening to your body for what it needs. He proceeds to try to convince me that the drinks and bars his nutritionist has him on contain everything he needs for his body.

I recall from his profile that he does martial arts, so I inquire which one he practices. Boxing. Ram shares from a now-that-I'm-older-and-wiser perspective, "It's not so much about knocking people out any more as when I was younger. But I'm not gonna lie, there is definitely a thrill in that still!" *Boo.* I am not a fan of violence, even in sport. *We are clearly not a good match for one another. However, I agreed to dinner because of his long drive and we have already ordered food, so I am going to stay and figure out how to not be miserable. I wonder if he thinks this date is going well? I wonder if I've come across in any peculiar ways on dates before. If I come across as crazy or as a control freak or exhibiting whatever "issues" that could be seen in a negative light.*

To bide my time, I decide to take on the role of interviewer, and learn as much about Ram as I can. I start by asking him what else he does for fun. He goes into detail about motorcycle racing, swimming with sharks, and bungee cord jumping. I recognize there's nothing wrong with any of these things, but it reinforces that a) he's an adrenaline lover, and b) we are not a good match.

The food arrives. Ram has a salad. With the dressing on the side.

I inquire about his work, which turns out to be very stressful. In the airline industry, he has been laid off, rehired, and is currently "terrified" of being laid off again. So much so, that he shares with me that he recently had to take some personal time off from his work, and was on temporary disability since he'd almost "lost his shit" on a coworker. *Oh, wow. That sounds serious. I'm not sure that this is the time for him to be dating.*

When I ask if he has done other work before he went into the airlines, Ram shares with me that he used to be a police officer in L.A. *Oh, goodness, if I had known that, I never would have dated him. Nothing wrong with it, but I don't think I'd date a man with a uniform, as they are constantly put in harm's way, and I'd worry too much.* I am pulled out of my thoughts as the conversation takes an interesting twist when Ram begins to talk about the dead people he encountered on his routes. I take a bite of my pasta, wondering how in the world he thinks it's okay to talk about that over dinner. *Everyone's different, but geez!* I can feel myself looking at him with a deadpan expression on my face as he finishes his story of this particular time that he thought his partner tapped him on the shoulder, but no, his partner was not even in the room. Just the dead body.

When I ask him about what he does for balance in his life, he mentions boxing again. I ask him if there are other things he does that chill him out rather than pump him up.

"What do you mean?" he asks.

"Well, like reading or hiking or meditating," I offer.

"I see what you are getting at. Well, you know I don't do those things. But, my family is from India, so I am spiritual. You know they do yoga there." *Well, yes, but...*

We both turn down dessert. For him, I'm going to make the assumption it's a calorie issue; for me, it's because I am beyond done with this date. When Ram invites me to go for a walk around the area, I decline. He insists on walking me back to my car. "After all, I was a police officer, and I know Oakland has some crime." Fortunately, I am parked close by. When he asks for another date, I say "yes," but for very different reasons than Chuck. Between his background as a boxer, a near breakdown at work, and what I'm making out to be potential control issues, I don't want to take any chances on a negative reaction to "no." *Being a woman, there are so many things to consider, especially when it comes to safety. I wonder if men ever feel this way?*

Then next day, I send a reconsideration text, thanking him for taking the time and energy to meet up, before adding him to my blocked numbers.

# SICK 'N' TIRED * MS. DYNAMITE

*I* *need to step back and reflect on this process, because boy, oh, boy, I am feeling* <u>done</u>*. Was my dream an illusion? Ultimately, I feel like I believe, but it's* <u>really</u> *hard to maintain faith sometimes. Especially after a dud of a date. How many times do I have to put myself out there? And, while I appreciate the many, seemingly endless options of online dating, I just don't think the Internet is how I'm going to meet my partner. At the same time, I do like feeling like I'm being proactive towards something I want to bring into my life. But is online dating worth all this effort and disappointment?*

Online dating seems to be a reflection of the world that we are living in where we check our phones continuously for texts and emails. Download movies instantaneously for our viewing pleasure. Get impatient if a web page is delayed two seconds when we press refresh. Order virtually any product we desire to be delivered to our door the next day. Get food to go without any time lapsed except to pull your car up to the next window. Upgrade to a new phone even though our old one still works just fine. In every pedicure parlor, what used to be a sanctuary is now a row of cell phone users. *It's no wonder that online dating parallels the instant gratification of the modern-day world, feeling like a mix between fast food and a video game.*

In some ways, online dating is like fast-food. There are lots of options, it's convenient, and it fills us up in the moment. However, the integrity of "ingredients" of the people we are about to "order" is not always what we think. Rather than quality, online dating relies on quantity. Daily, emails are sent with potential matches. Logging in, there are so many options to search through that I can spend hours upon hours at any given sitting, scrolling through countless people. I realize I am particular with eating, <u>and</u> with men, <u>and</u> with life in general. However, shouldn't there be a greater number of quality people who I actually want to go out with based on the hundreds I have reviewed? I <u>do</u> <u>not</u> want to go out with the man who writes "Am I cute? Yup! Am I sexy? Hell yeah!" or "I am merely a Romeo seeking a Shrew to tame" or other similar statements I have come across. *Wow, I am a bit fired up right now! But this is truly what it feels like sometimes! I don't want to eat fast-food, and I don't want to date these guys!*

To distract us from the fast-food-not-a-lot-of-quality nature of it, it seems like online dating uses certain features to make it resemble a fast-paced video game. I have the luxury of hitting a button to say "yes" or "no," which makes it feel less personal, and more like a game. The interface is set up like a dashboard. There are the features of favoriting, winking, and poking. The only thing missing is getting points, although I can see specifically who has viewed me, and how often, which could be viewed as points, I suppose. And yet, if I have had 500 views (or 50 for that matter) and I only get 2 messages what does this say to me? *Did I say something not cool? Did I include a picture that was too much or say something about myself that I did not want to say? Do I have some kind of cyber-spinach in my online teeth?*

Clearly feeling sick and tired about the whole online experience and trying not to be overwhelmed by it all, I decide to go to Rae's house. We both have stuff to work on, I feel like we both could use some girlfriend connection after my tirade and before I get back online to look for a date. Again. *How else will I find a date? How else will I find my partner?*

When I arrive, I share with Rae that I am not feeling very excited by the process. To her, online dating seems like it would be fun. (Note: she's been married for over 10 years, and has never had to do online dating herself.) Rae asks me some questions around my experience and is curious as to why online dating used to be more enjoyable for me. Reflecting on this, we conclude a) there seemed to be fewer crazies b) I was younger and perhaps less picky and c) I had a reward system for every first date I went on. Regardless of the date's success, I allowed myself to buy one pair of cute underwear for every first date I went on, so that there was a positive outcome each time. *Maybe I should try this reward system again? I am well stocked on undies, though. And, I don't want this to be a game any more than it already seems to be.*

A few minutes later, Rae looks over at me, with my furrowed brow of concentration and shares that she just realized that the process of looking for a new job and a new date are similar. For her job search, it comes down to things like being overqualified or underqualified, the pay being too low, not enough benefits, or too many hours. While the details for dating are obviously different, there is a similarity in terms of the degree of difficulty to finding a good fit. Rae and I chat further, and realize neither one of us is putting "positive energy" into our online research and wonder if perhaps that's contributing to feeling like we are getting bitten on our wireless asses. After all, how we view things and the power of intention we put into things really can make a big difference. We encourage each other to enter our searches with open minds and hearts.

# GET TO KNOW YOU * LEDISI

H aving clear, positive intentions, Aaron appears on my select-
ed potentials.

After the standard couple of emails back and forth, and a phone
conversation, we meet in person, to what is an immediate, strong attraction between us. A definite chemistry at play. I find myself wanting to get closer and maintain eye contact with some flirtatious looks
thrown in. *This is a rarity! Yay for staying open!*

In the midst of a flowing conversation, Aaron openly shares the
three potential deal breakers that I may have with him. He doesn't
want to waste my time, and likes to pride himself on his open, direct
communication, so he openly shares these parts of his past, in case
they make him a "no":

1.  He was arrested when he was younger for "suspicious behav-
    ior." This translates to tagging in NYC when he was a teenag-
    er. *Personally, I think this is pretty cool that he took the art form of his
    youth and found a way to use it in his adult life as a graphic designer.*
2.  He had been married. *I know it is more and more likely that the
    men I date will have already been married. My friend has a theory
    about how if men aren't married by their early 40s, they probably won't*

*get married. Not that it is impossible, just unlikely, as they have settled into their bachelor ways. I know, I know, you could say the same thing about a woman in her late 30s, right? Like I said, it's just a theory.* Aaron clarifies that he got married to help someone get citizenship. *For me, I have no issue with this either.*

3. In high school, his girlfriend got pregnant and had an abortion. *I stand strongly as a pro-choice woman.*

As we continue deep into conversation, I hear someone call out in a diva-esque voice, "Excuse me! Excuse me!" I turned around to see my beautiful esthetician. Since I never run into anyone I know in San Francisco, I am shocked to see her. She's an amazing woman, who knows a lot about me. A lot. Very intimate, personal details.

She starts telling her boyfriend and the bartender that she knew it was me because she recognized my voice (which is a bit on the husky side since I teach so much). "Her voice rules me!" Her enthusiasm makes me blush. It's almost like I planted her there on purpose to make me look good. Then, she turns and shares with her boyfriend, "Heather even has a special exercise in her class named after me." *Oh no. Please, please stop there.* She does, thankfully. It's a humbling position. And, something I don't want to explain on a first date. (Side Note: The exercise is to rest on the forearms with your booty raised up high in the air, like you are advertising your business to the whole world and then doing leg extensions up to the sky with a flexed foot. During our waxing sessions, the setup of this is done (without the leg extensions) in order for her to remove unwanted hair from a different angle.)

Aaron and I go out regularly over the next few weeks, taking one another to our favorite spots, sharing some amazing, quality time together, and getting closer each date. Things are flowing along nicely, and we're both making the effort to be together a few times a week. I am really, really liking him.

Then, I don't hear back from him for a week. *I am feeling a bit needy right now, which does not feel good.* I try to push aside the voice that there is something wrong, but it doesn't match the back-and-forth that we've had thus far. I go back to look at our text correspondence, and everything looks fine. I sent the last two text messages, so I decide not to send another. *I know you want to, but give it some space, Heather. Desperate is not a good look.* (REARVIEW MIRROR: Intuition is almost always right.)

When Aaron calls me the next day, he apologizes for the time that had gone by, reassuring me that he had been sick, applied for (and got!) a new job, and also had a cousin pass away. *Okay, cut him some slack. Don't be so hard. Basically, life happened. It would have been nice to share in those things as they happened, though, even though we haven't been dating that long. Ultimately, I want to have a relationship that has that, but maybe it's too early still.* I can't help push away the feeling like something has shifted.

The winter holidays are approaching, and we can't find a time to get together before I leave to see family out of town, so we leave it with a "let's text while I'm away" and plan a get-together as soon as I'm back in town.

While lounging at my parent's house, I come across a fascinating article on the brain. It reminds me of a conversation that I'd had with Aaron a few weeks prior, so I email it to him. He immediately writes a return email, asking if I am home yet from my trip. *That's sweet. He does want to see me.* I reply to let him know the date that I will return to the Bay, and propose getting together as soon as I get home, which happens to be the day of New Year's Eve.

However, I don't hear back. *What's going on here?*

I fly home at the end of the week, thinking that perhaps that is *it* with Aaron, which would really be too bad, but I stand resolute that I want to be with someone who equally wants to be with me and puts in the effort.

I celebrate New Year's Eve with good friends, and enjoy a hike in nature the following day, setting a new mantra for the year. This time it is: Release, with a special focus on the "ease" that goes with letting go of what does not serve. This includes Aaron.

A few days after the New Year, I receive a text from Aaron that simply reads, "Happy New Year!" *Huh? I thought he was gone. I am so not feeling the lapsed communication, but maybe this is something that we can talk about? It just feels like it shouldn't be an issue. Hmmm.*

I text back the same message with a confetti emoticon.

Nothing in return.

Like, nothing, nothing. *Okay, what in the world is going on here? His communication was so strong in the beginning. If you don't want to date me anymore for whatever reason, just let me know. Stop stringing me along!*

Instead, I am left wondering. And disappointed. Our time together was wonderful and we clearly both liked each other at the early stages of dating. I am left with the notion that some people are like those damn socks that get lost in the dryer. You know you washed both of them, but suddenly one is missing. Where the heck did it go?

# BLOW ME (ONE LAST KISS) * P!NK

I receive an email from the dating site as a "courtesy message" to let me know that men engage with women at a much higher percentage when they have been active on the site within 24 hours. I haven't been on since meeting Aaron. *I guess it's time to get back at it. Try, try again. Okay. But, seriously, I am not interested in being on the site every day. And, I'm not really interested in someone that is on it every day either. Seems like a bit of an addictive habit.* Trying to remember to have positive intentions, I log on and spend an hour sending replies to people.

I immediately hear back from Marcus, who looks promising.

After a couple of emails back and forth, he invites me to three venues of my choice that weekend. He clearly had done research by finding three live music options, which I very much appreciate. We land on a spot in the Mission neighborhood of San Francisco.

Marcus enters with a big smile, dressed smartly. We make our way to the bar to order wine in what turns out to be a very cramped venue. We decide to settle outside, due to the freestyle dancers, who look like they are doing a mix of a funky chicken and ode to the ocean waves without much regard for folks around them. *I love watching people move and being free, but it would be way too hard to have a first date conversation in the midst of this.* Because of the smoke, I feel a rare headache coming on and notice I am having challenges focusing. I find myself leaning sideways in my chair in an awkward manner to avoid touching the guy next to me. *This reminds me a bit of the Star Wars scene when the main characters are in the trash compactor. That's kinda funny, but I think I'm a little claustrophobic. I'm so not a fan of feeling cramped or trapped. Oh shit! Is this true of my relationships? Hmmm. Yes, perhaps with the men that are maybes when I agree to go out with them again. Not when they are a good fit like Aaron seemed to be.*

When Marcus walks me back to my car, he goes in for what I think is a hug. However, his lips are coming toward my mouth. Quickly. I drop my head to the right, and snake my body over as if I am doing a Soul Train dance move and let out an audible "Oooh!"

He exclaims, "Oh my gosh! I'm so sorry!" He seems embarrassed by the moment, sharing that he thought I'd given him a look that he chose to interpret as desiring more than just a hug. *Really?* With puppy-dog eyes and a goofy smile, he goes on to say, "I don't know you well enough to read your facial expressions yet." *I've been told that my face says it all. At the very least, I'm pretty sure it did <u>not</u> say, "Kiss me."* Marcus follows up by asking if he can make up for this date. Between the strange environments, the headache, and the almost-kiss, I can't decide where I stand with him. *He seems like a maybe, but with all these other factors, this one might need a second chance.* We set up a second date for the following week. (**REARVIEW MIRROR:** "Maybe's" are almost always "no's.")

Marcus arrives, carrying a bottle of sparkling wine. He remembered from my profile that I liked Prosecco, and the other venue didn't have any, so he brought some to make up for the last date. *Wow, how thoughtful and generous of him.*

The conversation is fine. Sadly, however, what is missing are any fireworks of attraction, which I suspected but couldn't fully tell from a first date that was filled with distractions. *While he seems like a really nice guy, clearly wants to be in a relationship, and to top it off, is attractive, the spark between us seems to be missing. Just because we are both single and both looking for a partner doesn't necessarily mean that we are a match for each other. It's too bad there's not the right chemistry, that va-va-voom that's hard to explain. But, I do know I need the va-va-voom.*

He walks me to my car as it starts to sprinkle. He comes in for what appears to be a hug.

And, without warning, I get licked across my cheek.

*What?*

I don't know exactly how it happened.

I could not reenact it for you.

Licked.

I am in complete shock.

As I attempt to back up from the hug that I've been caught in like a fish in the net, he doesn't notice my body language, and attempts to kiss/lick me again. *Just no.* Being licked feels very much like the experience of being dry humped by a dog. Both of you should be embarrassed, but only you, as the receiver, are. And, it certainly is not going to lead to anything. I do not mean to sound mean, but with the first attempted kiss and now this, I don't care if you were thoughtful enough to bring me bubbles and are a nice guy in general — under no early dating circumstances is it ever okay to lick someone without permission.

# BE OK * CHRISETTE MICHELE

My friend, Zia, wants to set me up with a guy she knows. She says Frank is younger, a "cool" kid with a big heart and ready for a relationship.

There ends up being a surprise birthday party for Zia the following week, and he is there. He doesn't make conversation or a lot of eye contact, so I am not sure whether or not he is interested.

As a follow-up, Zia lets me know that he is.

So, we meet up at a restaurant in Oakland and have a really nice chat. He is very passionate about his work, into martial arts, and a nice mix of serious and funny. He's also dapper in his attire.

After a stiff good-night hug, we set up another date. This time, we go to watch the sunset. He drives a sporty car and delves into his past being a bit rough when he was young. He brings wine, Spanish cheeses, and crackers. *So thoughtful.*

I am intrigued. Not blown away. But, intrigued.

Although we have only gone on two dates, New Year's is coming and I am wondering if I should ask him to be my date. While my comfort zone says I want to go to Rae's house with her and her husband and cook and watch the NYC ball drop, I decide to try something new.

So, Frank and I celebrate at the house of the friend who introduced us. Only, she didn't really know we were coming, as she was getting back from a retreat that day. So, there were four of us. It is fun, but a bit awkward. We end up going back to his place, even though it seems like he wants to go out to party. I am too old for this. He talks more about his hard childhood challenges. I sense there are a lot of unresolved issues.

For our next get-together, I invite Frank over to cook. He seems withdrawn. I ask him to talk about whatever is on his mind. He says it's him, that he has a lot going on, and is trying to deal with it. *Not a good sign. It is such a fine line between taking on other people's issues in this process, trying to make a deep connection and protecting myself at the same time.*

I invite him to a concert the following week. He does not want me to pick him up; he prefers to meet there. He does not want any food; he just wants a drink, which he pays for without offering to pay for mine. It's just awkward.

I drive him home, and he says he will call to make plans.

He doesn't. I also don't follow-up.

Sometimes, it's clear when someone is working on their shit. I have to ask myself: Is this my shit or your shit? If it's mine, let me attend to it. If it's yours, you deal with it, and let me not take it on. *Dating requires so many different types of filters that you have to test against your intuition.*

# TELL ME SOMETHING GOOD
# RUFUS FEAT. CHAKA KHAN

When I tell my mother of my recent goodbye to Frank, some other dating woes, as well as some updates on one of my childhood friends who is also going through some hard times in her relationship, she shares, "You know, Heather, it's really too bad you ladies aren't lesbians. You already love each other, respect and make sense to one another. It's already a healthy long-term relationship in so many important ways. Wouldn't it be nice if you could just move in together and keep each other company? You could have your businesses together. And, then we could have kids in the family."

This is coming from my mother, who, as a single woman in the '60s, moved to Morocco to be a teacher. My mom, who was still single at an "older" age than most ladies of that time; my mom, who reached a point and attitude where she was perfectly fine being on her own and not being with a man. My mom, who started taking ballet with me at the age of 40 and even made it to be on pointe! My mom, who taught for decades, helping countless children become better people. My mom, who raised me and I am so thankful for. My mom, who just said I should become a lesbian, because I can't find a relationship with a man! And let me be clear, while I think women are spectacular, I don't find myself having romantic or sexual feelings for them, but you know if I did, I wonder if it might be easier to find my Mrs. Right.

Clearly, what she was really saying is she wants me to be in a fulfilling relationship.

It has taken me a long time to get to the place where I am now accepting of myself as a single lady. From age 13, I remember taking epic drives to visit our family in the summertime. As a kid, these drives felt they never ended. The phrase, "Are we there yet?" was used often. One of the things I remember from those drives was spending time thinking about my Mr. Right. Especially when we would drive at sunset and the view of the passing country was beautiful. Purplish mountainsides. Trees that were in endless patterned lines. Clouds that were constantly impressed me with their varying beauty and yet their essence remained the same. *How is it that even as a young girl, I internalized some message that this is the way to happiness?*

I still fantasize about my love. I light a tea-candle almost every night that is housed in a Moroccan lantern by my window to call my love in. Maybe fantasy is way too superficial a word for what I imagine. In fact, somewhere along the way, I have come to hold a deep faith in love. In fact, as my acceptance of myself has grown and my connections with those in my life have strengthened, I have never been more certain about the power and reality of love.

I will say that I am thankful that I am where I am. While the essence of me is the same, I feel as though I have grown so much as a person. I feel like I am more comfortable being single. I have figured out how to be independent. Seriously, if I had been married and had a child when I was younger, I don't think I would have become the person I am. I am thankful for loving who I have grown into. As one of my friends recently said about evolving, "I have grown so eff-ing much. I should be as tall as the Jolly Green Giant by now!" I feel the same.

# YOU'RE NOT THE MAN * SADE

J uly 4. A day known by some in this country to be about fireworks. It also happens to be the day my Internet dating sub-
scription is up.

*What to do? Renew or let go? Besides Aaron, the missing sock in the dryer,
there has not been anyone else I want to get to know better. And, with a few
experiences, including the unsolicited licking that clearly did not sit well with
me, it may be time to sign off. Well, let me take one more look to see if there are
any prospects and maybe then I'll be done for this round.*

When I log on, I choose to focus on the list of folks the website
recommends specifically for me. I've done it a few times before, but
normally I just reply to people that write to me. *Although I am not sure
how they figure out the likelihood that we will be compatible, I kind of like this
approach.* Regardless of how unsuccessful it's been so far, I press the
button and search.

At the very tip top of the list, numero uno, there he is with 100%
compatibility.

100%.

It's a rare thing to find someone that is that high, the highest of highs. In fact, in my on-and-off relationship with online dating, I don't think I have <u>ever</u> gotten a match that's a perfect 100%. *Is this even possible?*

Reading the profile, everything on paper, or "on screen," looks to be in place and appears to meet everything I'm looking for. He's athletic, smart, generous (the "rock" in his friendships), witty (comments that would ordinarily make me giggle out loud from reading his profile), steady (secure job), and really handsome (pure chemistry). He seems to be the perfect blend of a strong man with a big heart and a smart mind.

The only part that my Spidey senses detect as a potential issue is that he shares that he lives life fully: "If you are going to go all out it's with 100 percent. Conversely when you make a mistake, you should do that with gusto as well." *Hmmm. While I try to learn from all my mistakes too, I don't necessarily want to highlight them as such an achievement or shout them from the top of a mountain. I want to learn from them, and move on.*

Everything else looks good.

Except I know him. Knew him. It's my Ex. The one who broke my heart. Seeing him makes my heart race a bit faster. But, most definitely no fireworks anymore. It feels like there is a carnival mirror on my computer screen that is reflecting him back to me, making him seem distorted. I hold my breath as I block him. Then, I close down my profile.

July 4th. The day I get off Internet dating. Again.

# NO MORE DRAMA * MARY J. BLIGE

The next week, I receive an email from Aaron, the missing sock in the dryer. *What in the world? This is certainly unexpected. What will he say?* I click to open it. It reads:

Soooooooooooooo, yeah. It's been a long time since we have spoken/communicated. There's a reason for that...I'm hoping we could meet up and maybe have a drink or a bite and talk, even if you moderately dislike me at the moment. You are welcome to totally disregard this email, but, I'm hoping you'll respond : ) Peace and Love, Aaron

*What does this mean?*

In my experience, getting back together with people doesn't work. It reminds me of when I learned to drive a stick shift in high school in my dad's car. On one occasion, I took a different route, and came to a small hill on my drive from my house to the base. I couldn't get the balance quickly enough between the gas and the clutch and I rolled back. All the way back to the bottom of the hill. I chose to go a different way. Sometimes life can be like this too. There are times you find yourself rolling backward, even though you want to go forward. With dating in particular, however, I have found going back isn't ever fruitful. Moving forward is the best option.

That being said, it's one thing to know something in <u>theory</u>; another to feel and live it. While my inclination is that it isn't a good idea to re-explore with Aaron, there had not been anything wrong with the budding relationship that we had started, except that he stopped showing up. I feel a small glimmer of hope, so I respond with a short email, letting him know that I was open to a conversation. (REARVIEW MIRROR: If someone disappears and wants to come back, just say no.)

I am met with a follow-up email that highlights how he missed me, he thought about me a lot, and he had a strong desire to be friends. *Friends? Why didn't he say that in his initial email?*

When I was younger, I tried to be "friends" after a breakup. The outcomes were usually one of the following:

- You end up getting back together, which, in my experience, was never a positive thing, because the shit that broke you up in the first place is still there. Only this time, after the initial lovey-dovey phase is over, you are kicking yourself a bit harder in the tushie for thinking it would somehow be different this time around.
- One of you has feelings for the other, even when you claim you don't and the dynamics of the relationship are hella off.
- You become friends. However, this one has eluded me so far, as it always been my experience that someone always still *likes* someone. I have witnessed a few successes with other people in my life, but mostly it's because one or both people get married, so the boundary is clear.

For me, I've learned when it's over, it's time to say good-bye, and take some time to reflect on lessons I've learned, keep a warm spot in my heart for the good memories, and try to let go of that person.

*But, where does the love or adoration go when you decide not to be together? Does it continue to live within your heart? Does it become a memory, tied only to the past where the mind can visit? Does it transform like magic from caterpillar to butterfly to move you forward to what comes next? Where does the love go? Does it just disappear? And, how about when you didn't choose to say goodbye, but the choice is made by the other person?*

I write Aaron back with a "best of luck" email.

# I CAN'T MAKE YOU LOVE ME * ADELE

S haring my most recent dating misadventures with Chantal, she tells me that she wants me to meet her housemate, Mike. She has thought about telling me several times, because it keeps popping up in her head that we'd make good match. To be real, I am not particularly interested in dating someone far away (he lives in Pacifica, a little under an hour from Oakland, if the traffic is favorable) or who lives in a household of women. *No judgment. Well, actually, maybe some. Okay, I'll own it. I'd prefer to date someone who has his own space and lives locally at this point in my life. Is it true that as we get older, we become more set in what we want?*

The next time I go visit Chantal, Mike opens the door. My heart literally takes a leap. Beyond butterflies. There is something about our chemistry that is simply undeniable.

In a situation where the introduction comes through a mutual friend, there is a certain amount of trust that exists from the beginning. Internet dating is so different, as you have no idea about who your dates are. When the person comes with a friend's "reference check," it feels so much more valid. And, when you add in sparks that are flying, it's all systems go!

After spending part of the day with both Chantal and Mike, I head back home, bubbling with excitement. Chantal texts me the next day to ask if it is all right to pass my number on to him. YES!

And, then nothing. *Why isn't he calling?*

After a week, I call Chantal and I ask about it. She says she doesn't know why Mike hasn't called.

A few weeks later, I head back to Pacifica to visit her again. Of course, I am hoping to see him as well.

While Chantal is in the kitchen making lunch, Mike comes into the living room to talk with me. After our initial hello, he dives straight into how he realizes that he asked for my number and then didn't follow up. *Hmm, okay, so I didn't misread this connection.*

"Yes, I was wondering about that," I respond, trying to sound casual.

He explains to me that he's in "transition," meaning he is most likely leaving in a month to go home for the summer in order to figure out life and his next steps. He thinks he wants to change his career path back to being a firefighter. He doesn't think this is the best time to be in a relationship with the uncertainty in his life. I understand. Yet, I also believe that sometimes things come into our lives, and we have to pay attention.

I share, "In my experience, it's rare to find someone that you want to talk about being in a relationship with the second time you meet them. We have to be open to possibilities."

"I totally hear you," he replies. "You are absolutely right."

We end up hanging out for the rest of the day. *Butterflies.*

He comes to visit me in Oakland. We have a beautiful time making lunch together, walking in the rose garden and sitting by Lake Merritt. Just being in his presence makes me feel peaceful and fully alive. I am completely myself with Mike. I have moments of depth and silliness and inquisitiveness. *It's interesting when I go on first dates with guys I don't know. I am still myself, but I'm definitely more guarded and less goofy than I am in real life when people know me. It is nice to show up as my full, authentic self.*

After a month, I become aware that while I really, really like Mike, I am the one who is trying to push forward to know him better. I set up times to meet, call him, and send him care packages with photos of clouds and CDs for inspiration. Basically, I am wooing him. While he responds to my actions, he doesn't take initiative to do anything on his own. *Sure, he told me the first time we met that he was not in a position to be available. I was equally convinced at that time that because of the unique magical feeling, maybe I was his "one" and could show him he was ready. That spending time together would change his mind. What is it about me that I didn't listen to what he said? When people tell you who they are, you need to believe them. It really is about both people being in a space where they are willing and able to put energy into making it work. But, I really like him. I don't want to let go. But, I can't hold on. The truth of it is you can't make people love you.*

# I WANT A LITTLE SUGAR IN MY BOWL
## NINA SIMONE

A pause for an almost-love.

A pause to focus on just living.

Spring cleaning my house, feeling good. Creating space for newness by clearing out my closets. And drawers.

Only to find...

Condoms.

Expired.

*Damn, it's been awhile. Where does the time go?*

# I TRY * MACY GRAY

Deciding to take another break from dating, I set up meetings with a bunch of my girlfriends who have recently navigated the dating scene. While there are deeper reflections that parallel my thinking about maintaining faith in love, there are many stories that make me laugh or shake my head in disbelief at the absurdity of certain dating scenarios. Here are the highlights from the crème de la crème from their experiences.

Imagine. He:

- is overheard working with a dating coach in the grocery store, practicing what to say, before approaching you to ask about the brand of yogurt in your basket.
- smiles at you in the grocery store, and then finds you in the parking lot, with a prominent erection that is visible through his white soccer shorts.
- lives in the same building as you and while in the elevator, he picks up your laundry (without knowing the status of cleanliness) and smells it, before asking you on a date.
- tells you that he knew he had to approach you from the front, as he didn't know what would happen if he approached you from behind "with a booty like that."

In the initial interaction, he:

- lists himself as a "street pharmacist" or a "medical service provider" as an alternative way of saying he is a drug dealer.
- shares with you that his "biological clock" is ticking. He has three young children with three different women who are all born within a year of each other.
- asks you if you are "domestic."
- texts you before a first date: "I just want to make sure you are coming before I cross the bridge and have to pay the toll."
- messages you before the first date, scheduled later that night, to tell you that his ex has "cluhmideeah" and he needs to reschedule.
- sends you a photo of his penis, with an empty toilet paper roll next to it, so you can see its proportions.

On a first date, he:

- has gotten tribal facial tattoos since his profile pictures were taken.
- rear-ends your car after a not-so-great first date, and then refuses to give you his insurance information, but happily offers to give you free massages.
- confesses that he is stretching out his foreskin to help increase his sensitivity, and he has built his own weight device to help with the process.
- explains to you he had a foot issue when he was younger, then proceeds to remove his shoe in the restaurant to show you how it still affects him.
- noticeably looks you up and down a couple of times, giving you a visible head nod of approval, and then tells you he's looking for the "perfect mix of G.I. Jane and Barbie" and you're a fit.
- packs himself an overnight bag which he brings into the restaurant.

- proudly tells you he is going to get a tattoo and it will be so awesome because it is in "code." When you guess that B2TW stands for "balls to the wall," he is mystified that you figured it out.
- breaks down, saying he's still in love with his ex-girlfriend, even though he's been sleeping with his housemate. Then, the next day, tries to connect with you on LinkedIn.
- pulls out a coupon at the end of the date. It's for buy one meal, get one free. Then, proceeds to tell you the free one is for him, so you have to pay for your own.
- yells, "BA-BAM! It's like that! BA-BAM! Just pulling out two $20s! That's how you roll. BA-BAM! Forty dollars!" when you put your portion of the bill on the table.
- quips, "You gonna go drop a deuce?" when you excuse yourself to the bathroom.

After a couple of dates, he:

- (tries to) slyly cover up his ring finger (surprise!) with a receipt so you can't see the wedding band when you run into him at the store.
- has home decor that includes a planter decorated with a pair of women's white lacy undies with a butterfly for aesthetics.
- applies deodorant in the convenience store (and puts it back on the shelf) when you stop for gas.
- tells you he has "man toys" in his closet. They turn out to be action figures (Superman, X-Men, etc.) in the original packaging.
- urinates in the bed the first time you sleep over, and does not say anything about it.
- eats a huge plate of pie and ice cream, only to inform you that he is lactose intolerant and you'll have to drive with the windows down.

- says he is too tired to talk, and that he'd prefer to talk the next day. Then, he calls a month later to ask you what you wanted to talk about.

Here's the thing: all these snippets are from women who are professional, beautiful, intelligent, creative, and available. While, <u>yes</u>, we all have things to "work on" as well as expectations and assumptions to inspect, and layers to peel back, the reality is that part of this dating experience is also just some crazy-ass shit! For every one successful story, there are <u>at least</u> ten doozies. *Dating is such an interesting road to navigate, and I am beyond appreciative for the reminder that I am, indeed, <u>not</u> alone.*

# SUGAR MAMA * BEYONCÉ

When my friend Patricia sets me up on a blind date with a guy named Elijah, I am thrilled. Not only a date, but another real-life connection. *This is most definitely my preference in dating!*

Patricia had met Elijah a few times in a casual group setting and thought he'd be a great match for me. We are both in the fitness industry. She thinks he's handsome. And, Patricia informs me that she made sure Elijah has no attachments to other women and is ready to date seriously. *It's funny that I still have a bit of a sore spot around other women. I never cared about that before my Ex. I wonder if I'll be able to let that go fully. I hope so.*

Elijah told Patricia that he was happy to proceed forward in whatever manner I was most comfortable with: he can call me or I can call him. *How thoughtful! It sounds old-school, but I really prefer when the man takes the lead on this, so I tell her to please have him call me.*

Elijah sends me a text, and we land on chatting on the phone the following day.

I end up driving to San Jose to look at a car to replace my old one (a single lady adventure in and of itself). When he texts to see if I am available, I apologize, letting him know that it'll be a bit longer because I am buying a car.

After an unexpectedly long day, I text Elijah before heading back to Oakland, "Are you available to chat now?"

His text reply is: "Yes."

I decide to call him rather than continue with the back-and-forth texts, even though I initially wanted him to call me. *I know, I know, let it go! But, is it indicative of actions not matching the words? He texted. He said he would call. Oh my God! You are being ridiculous! You were the one who couldn't talk earlier. You are so overthinking this!*

During our chat, I learn about a few things that he likes, but I am not a huge fan of: camping being one of them. (Don't get me wrong, I like being in nature. I very much enjoy hiking. I also like a real bed. And an accessible, private, clean bathroom that does not require a flashlight or carry the risk of being met by a wild animal.) This detail is not at all a deal-breaker, just a mental note. He's also a huge sports fan. Again, not a huge deal, as long as I don't have to go to a lot of games. *I wonder if there are things he is noting about me as well. She said the word glitter. (Insert buzzer noise.) She likes to dress up and go to fancy places. (Insert Casino slot machine noise.) I mean really, aren't we all, in some ways, sizing each other up with the goal of trying to figure out if we would make a good match?*

Elijah and I meet the next evening at a tapas restaurant. I am legitimately excited to meet him in person. After I park, I text that I am the girl sitting at the bar with a red sweater and a flower in my hair, since we've never met or even seen a photo of each other. Blind dates require even more James Bond, or Jane Bond sleuthing skills to try to figure out who the other person is. He texts back that he has on a blue shirt and is walking through the door.

As he walks over to me, I stand up. He hugs me. *I find it interesting how there are hugs exchanged at the beginning of first dates. I don't know you yet or vice versa. We may never see each other again. Heather, stop! Just enjoy the moment.*

After hugging, he immediately comments that he really likes Spanish food, as his ex-girlfriend was Spanish. *Oh boy.* Mentioning an ex within 30 seconds of meeting, before our behinds are even in the chairs, is a new record in my book.

The conversation that follows is fine. We have a lot to talk about since we are in a similar line of work. I decide halfway through that while he feels like "maybe," I'd be open to going on a second date, to see which way the maybe leans, as it currently seems to be split down the middle.

The waiter brings the check, which he places directly next to Elijah.

Elijah looks at me point blank, asking, "Do you find it odd when the waiter puts the check by the man?"

I look back at him, and reply, "No."

There is an awkward pause, as if he is not expecting this answer, and he looks away.

"I'm happy to chat about why," I tell him.

"No, no," he says, "I was just curious."

I pull out my hot pink clutch and proceed to take out a $20 bill to pay for my half; the check in its entirety for both of us is $30. (REARVIEW MIRROR: If there appears to be an uncomfortable difference of opinion between two people that are interested in each other, be sure that a conversation can happen. This way you can hear each other's perspectives and weed out any potential underlying assumptions.)

Here's a little more context, even though I didn't get to share it with Elijah: I grew up with an older brother who I had to share a lot with, most notably desserts. My mother, being a clever teacher, gave my brother and me each a job; one person split the food and the other got to choose which half he or she wanted. While I realize things in life are not so clearly 50/50, it goes back to my dating equation where there should be an overall balance. I <u>totally</u> realize that this is old-fashioned, or maybe it's a universal, unspoken dating rule, and we may disagree on this point, but this is what it means to me:

- You offer to pay and I accept = we both would like to go on another date.
- You offer to pay and I thank you, but offer to pay your own portion more than once = I am not interested.
- You don't offer to pay, and we split the check = you (or both of us) are not interested.

He walks me to my car, and says that he'd like me to think about if I'd like to go out again. I inform him that I am interested. He repeats again that I should think about it, and I again state that I am interested (mentally noting that he is not listening, or perhaps he is not interested in a second date based on the check situation.) *Well, now, maybe I don't want a second date. But, Patricia really thought we'd hit it off.*

A week later, I do not hear from him. Another missing sock in the dryer perhaps.

Two weeks later, I meet up with Patricia, who says she just got a text from Elijah asking for my number, saying he had lost it. At this point, my maybe became a no. *I know my expectations for my partner might seem high, but they should be. I'm a grown-ass woman. If you are truly interested, there is none of this bullshit. If you like me, call me. No waiting. No games. No losing numbers and waiting two weeks to ask for it again. I would rather stay single than be with someone who isn't right. This dating thing is really getting me to be clear about boundaries and identify and dismiss bullshit a whole lot faster. It is also forcing me to practice patience. What I want is worth it.*

# PIECES OF ME * LEDISI

W hen I was eight, I recall standing in line with my dad to get an ID card, bored to tears. Noticing my antsy-ness, he said to me, "You know, Heather, you are going to have to learn this thing called patience. Otherwise, it's going to be a hard life." *Funny how certain memories stay strong.*

While I wish that I could have somehow taken that lesson into my mind and heart at that young age, and been more Zen from that moment forward, it's been one of those lessons I have needed to work through time and time again. From simple things like the instant gratification of shopping, to bigger challenges like spending the majority of my life being stressed about finding "the one." On the dating continuum, I slide between being fine and allowing what will be, to being all the way to the other end of the spectrum - FUCK! Where are you already?! *I do feel like I am learning to trust in the process more, even though I have my moments. I feel like I've been trying for so long to figure this whole relationship thing out. Time is flying by! I'm almost 39! While I am finding that in some ways dating is easier, it also feels harder, or at least different, than when I was younger, mostly due to the aging process.*

In the spirit of openness, I share:

Let's start with the gray hair situation. While the first one was a bit alarming, it was easy enough to pluck it out. Eventually there were a few more. Then, I noticed the few "randoms" grew into a small colony. These days, <u>somehow</u>, I find myself at a stop light with tweezers, using the natural light to pluck one out. I've become one of "those" people, crossing to the other side as if I am invisible just because I am in my own car. *I am plucking out a gray hair. With tweezers. At a stoplight.* I call and make an appointment to add blond highlights to my naturally light brown hair in order to camouflage them like a chameleon, blending my way into notions of youthfulness. And, while I do it for myself, I also must be totally honest in sharing that I am mindful about how men will perceive me as "older" because of grays, perhaps less desirable, and think my expiration date is coming up. *Just being real.*

Besides the grey hairs, there is another "hairy" situation. It seems we start getting more hair in some not-so-opportune places. One above the lip. A random chin one. And, they are courser too. I mean, what the eff? I have even bared witness to a few on my upper leg that were never there before (most of the rest of it is baby blond hair, which I am thankful for). Annoying would be one word for it. While I know that it does not make me less womanly, it is a physical shift that changes my perception about my public presentation of self. It's also an internal wondering that impacts feeling desirable.

Next, we have skin. While there are still periods in which I get "zots" (as my dad calls them), there are also the wrinkles. The fine lines, the laugh line, the animation lines, the story of my life a.k.a. wrinkles. While Hollywood airbrushing and Botox would have us believe otherwise, the reality is: gravity happens. Expressions that we practice with regularity, sleep patterns and genetics put perm-a-lines on our faces that deepen with time. I have tried many different creams, but it is what it is. More things to see in the mirror when preparing for a date. While I try not to pay too much attention, it's in the background for sure. *At least I'm proud to say, my deepest lines seem to be from laughing and smiling!*

There is also the "issue" of the cottage cheese look that appears out of nowhere on certain parts of the body. It does not matter how many butt exercises I do or what I eat, cellulite is inevitable for most women. While this one is less of an issue for me at this point, as I have not been naked with anyone in quite some time and bathing suits have been worn only with my girlfriends, it is still another shift in how I relate to my body. *It's been so long since I've been with someone, I wonder if I will feel different about my body in that regard as well. Am I still sexy?*

As if these more superficial realities aren't enough, there are also changing energy levels. Even with healthy eating and the right combination of supplements, I just don't have quite the same vivacious energy level as kids on the playground. This leads to things like sneaking in cat naps. *Seriously, yay for naps!* It also makes going out at 5 p.m. for Happy Hour a better option than dinner at 9 p.m. at a new, posh restaurant. Or, choosing to stay in instead of going out at times. This ties into recovery times as well. Workouts take a bit longer to rev up for and staying up late or drinking alcohol takes longer to recover from. If you are in your 40s and still want to go clubbing until 2 a.m., I wish you the best, but you're on your own with that one.

And, then, there are the changing hormones. First off, can I please put in a request to the Universe that we really don't need so many periods? How about once a season? That feels about right to me. And, speaking of periods, hormones, and age...

My biological clock is ticking. I have always wanted a child, and thought I'd have one by now. After the end of my last disastrous relationship with my Ex was the first time that I shifted and thought about the possibility of <u>not</u> having a child. Perhaps our breakup was extra hard because his daughter was involved. Our disentanglement also involved my heart's connection to her. My heart was broken a little more because of it. Since then, I have a hard time checking the dating profile box (have kids, want kids, don't want kids). Checking those boxes is already a charged issue. What about an "I-don't-know-anymore" box? It's not that I am ambivalent about it, but as I get older, the issue is so much more complicated. To be real, it also depends on if I can even have one. My acupuncturist recently asked me if I was planning to have kids. She immediately blurted out how I may want to consider freezing my eggs. I told her that this option did not interest me. I think at this point, I want my focus to be on meeting my partner. And, things will work out as they need to. If I have a child, awesome; if I don't, well, it will be a path less taken, but it'll be okay too. The scary part is that at a certain point, I will no longer have the choice.

*From grey hairs to whether or not I want to have a baby, getting older is a freakin' trip, especially when still dating and searching for love!*

Getting older is also beautiful and amazing in many ways. We get to learn how to drop into who we are more (mostly) unapologetically. We still have thoughts that don't serve us but it's easier to catch them, and say, "Fuck it! I'm fabulous!" We get to accept ourselves more authentically. We are able to enjoy the small things in life more fully. We have a deeper understanding of how precious life is, and that each second is a gift. We realize that this is it. No more living in fantasyland waiting for "things" to come into our lives to be happy. Yes, we still dream but know that happiness is largely ours to create. In an attempt to live a life that is flying by, we slow down a bit and are not in such a hurry anymore. Where is there to go but here? We breathe in and into the moments that make up our stories.

One of my tattoos is Cantonese for "beautiful flower." It serves as a reminder that things unfold in their own time, beautifully, and you cannot force the bud to open any quicker than it is ready to. An ongoing lesson to recall as I navigate my life in general, and specifically my world of being single. **Let go, stop fighting the flow of the current, and trust that the process will unfold**. Even when you are unsure. In fact, I think that's the point.

# I AM WOMAN * JORDIN SPARKS

Valentine's Day, aka Hallmark day. It's just a day like any other, but can carry some weight, especially for single folks.

I teach a dance class that night, sharing the evening with my ladies. I purchase toy engagement rings to use to propose to ourselves, and we do a Soul Train line to "Sign, Sealed, Delivered" by Stevie Wonder. It is a wonderful celebration of women being women for the sake of ourselves, making a commitment to love ourselves always.

As I drive home, I reflect on how lucky I am to have so many incredible women in my life and how fortunate I am to do the work I do. I cannot wait to get home for my night in: a glass of champagne and a special bubble bath with a bath bomb that makes the water a luminous purple, smell of lavender. I put on cute lingerie, just for myself, and make an art collage.

*The transformation is tangible: I love looking forward to being on my own. Alone with myself, but not lonely. Full. Present. Loved. Authentically me. I am loving the practice of loving me. Of creating my own joy.*

# BREAKTHROUGH * JAZZYFATNASTEES

The next day as I walk out of the pharmacy with Rae, I am carrying a big bag of dance gear strapped over my shoulder, two grocery bags (one in each arm) and a jumbo pack of toilet paper tucked under my left arm. Rae offers to carry my toilet paper or a bag. "I'm fine," I assure her. She looks at me knowingly, and says, "You know, Heather, you don't always have to be so independent. It's okay for other people to help you."

At first I protest, as I do not see anything wrong with how I am operating. This is simply how I function: I do this plus go up the two flights of stairs to my house all the time. I avoid making multiple trips whenever possible. However, as I am telling her "It's all good…" I realize that I am indeed balancing a lot, and she is empty-handed, offering help. I hand her the toilet paper. She pauses and then firmly yet lovingly asserts, "You might apply this lesson to your dating life too."

I am struck by this. Yes, I have become very independent. Not just with my toilet paper, but with most things in general. Perhaps elements of me have always been that way. But, for sure, I've become this way because I've had to. *How can I be so fiercely independent yet still want so much to find my partner? It's like trying to mix old fairy tales of love and happily ever after with what it means to be a modern day woman!*

Thinking about this, I call Anna that night and I tell her the toilet paper story. We both laugh at the simplicity of the story and the complicated nature of its implications. When she asks me about what's happening in my dating life, I tell her I'm in a dry spell. I reference "my list," and have an ah-ha moment in which I realize that my list is really all in my head. The last actual list I wrote was in 1999! (Now I have Prince's "Gonna Party Like it's 1999" in my head!). Anna suggests we make a date to update my list. *What purpose does a list even serve? When I was younger, it had some things that were not as critical as I do now. Does it really help to clarify what is at the core of what we want?*

My initial hesitation to rewriting it is that I know I am particular. Some may even call it picky. So, how can I get outside of my boxes? My 1999 brainstorm list had three categories: Must Be, Non-negotiable and Negotiable. Interestingly, many of them are still true. Things like kind, ambitious, healthy. *But, what do these things really mean? What do they look like, sound like, feel like? My version of "kind" might be very different than someone else's version.* A few have become more clear now. For example, "has a healthy confidence, maintains solid friendships, respects being faithful, and is ready for commitment".

Enlisting Anna's help, we decide not to have any boxes or lines. Instead, I write the word "LOVE" in the middle of my paper and draw a heart around it with a bunch of offshoots. We do a brainstorm together. The easier ones flow out, and I write them down quickly. Anna helps me find clarity with many of them. We talk through the meaning behind the ones I feel I am being too picky about to find the right wording. Being specific yet open. The page becomes filled with words that represent what I desire to bring in. *Maybe this will help.*

I join another dating site. This one has been a reputation for being more "serious."

# WE ALL WANT LOVE * RIHANNA

O n this new site, I start corresponding with a guy named Eric who looks nice.

For our first date, he recommends grabbing a drink at a cool new spot in Oakland that I've been wanting to try. A funky place with brick walls filled with notes in the various cracks.

Eric texts me to let me know he's arrived 30 minutes early and is going to order himself food. I show up on time, and find him fully grubbing on pizza. He stands up, a napkin dropping to the ground, mouth full of food. *He seems very comfortable with himself.* He explains that he didn't know how traffic would be, so he decided to arrive on the earlier side. Plus, he'd been wanting to try the food here anyway while respecting our "just drinks" date.

Eric grabs his plate from the bar, and we walk over to a vacant table to order drinks. As he continues to eat, we have a good chat on various topics. At the end, I am more than happy to accept a second date. It's partially because of his cuteness and partly his comfort with himself.

Eric arranges the next date in the city at a place that's so trendy that it doesn't even have its name on a sign, just the address. The line is unbelievably long. He informs me that he has not eaten all day in anticipation of eating there. We are seated at the community table, close to a door that opens and closes regularly. I order one dish. He orders four.

He eats. A lot. He barely looks up from his food. Due to the high volume of noise from the crammed-in customers and his focus on food in front of him, there is minimal conversation between us. So, I watch him eat. *This guy is a serious foodie! I like to eat food too, but he takes it to a whole new level!* When he is "slightly beyond full," Eric gets the rest of his food wrapped up to take with him, and we walk a few blocks away to a famous ice cream spot. On our walk, he grabs my hand, and tells me that he really likes me and he is so happy to go on this "perfect" date.

On our next date, we have dinner at a mutually favorite Indian restaurant. I am again impressed by how much food he consumes. *This guy lives for food. And, he gets absolutely lost when he is eating. Nothing else seems to exist.* The date ends with a hard-lipped kiss. *He is attractive for sure, but something is missing. Or, was it just an awkward first kiss?*

But, he's very nice. And, I am trying to be open to possibilities. *It's not looking good, though. Haven't I learned that the maybe's are usually no's? But, he's really nice and cute. Let me try one more time!*

That weekend, Eric and I meet for a movie. He offers to come out to meet me at the parking lot as it is not the best area and the lot is dark. *He's so thoughtful.* As the movie begins, he takes my hand to hold, and starts to stroke it. Like non-stop. Like annoying. I am so distracted by this repetitive motion that I can't focus on the movie. *Shoot, shoot, shoot! If such basic things feel off, chemistry in the bedroom would most likely be off too.* About halfway through the movie, I think his thumb must be getting tired but it does not. So, I let go of feeling like a bitch, and very slowly do a slow-motion thumb-wrestling maneuver to pin down his thumb. The stroking finally stops. The date ends in another hard kiss, as he shares that it has been yet another "perfect" date. "Perfect," and yet, we hardly did any talking.

Via text, he informs me that his folks are in town the following week and he wants me to meet them. *Already?* He clearly feels more strongly about me than I do about him, and I need to say goodbye, as I don't think my feelings will grow. We are both looking for love. However, sadly, just because someone is a good person and fits the criteria on your list, doesn't mean he is the "one." I know he will find someone. I hope I will too. *What is it that I can't capture on a list about my partner that is beyond a list? And, what do I need to do to find him? Desire to connect, let it go, desire to love, let it go. I don't know what else to do! Moments of clarity, of knowing and moments of feeling crazy and hopeless. What do I need to do differently? What is this intense drive to find my partner even about?*

# HIGHER THAN THIS * LEDISI

**M**editation has always seemed like such a good way to take care of myself. I've had the best intention to start a practice. I just never really have enough time. You know: a few minutes of extra sleep in the morning. The emails are calling. I need to see what is going on in the world, so I turn on the news. The dishes really should get done before they pile up. All of a sudden, it is time to go to work, so I fly down the stairs quickly to start the day from this hurried place, promising to try again tomorrow.

When I've tried meditating before, my mind has been so busy I've felt like I've spent the entire time thinking about what I am thinking. This did not feel "right." In fact, it felt like the antithesis of what I was trying to achieve, which was some kind of ambiguous, "higher," blissful, peaceful state. While I do not expect to levitate, I do expect something magical to occur. As is the case with most things in life, if you don't feel successful, you don't usually want to do them.

My massage practice is growing, and I find myself time and time again able to be present for my clients. For their healing. I can be in the mode of go, go, go, and before a client comes, I am still able to center myself and show up. It's like a moving meditation. I find myself fully in the moment, with a groundedness and balance that come from a different kind of listening. Like hearing the ocean inside of a seashell.

In talking with my massage teacher, I share how I can intuitively feel when I come to a spot on someone's body that needs particular attention. These spaces either call for holds to fill the emptiness or holds that provide permission to release. When I encounter these spaces, I feel tears behind my eyes. She listens, then tells me that perhaps I have reached a point in my practice where it is time to consider teaching. Quickly, I dismiss the idea. I don't feel ready.

In dance classes, I am in the present as well. When I move, I feel alive. When I feel alive, I take notice of what is happening around me. Within the contexts of my classes, this means noticing the ladies that have come to dance with me. Together, we express emotions that are beyond words through dance. Thoughts about the day disintegrate, past and future are not pondered on, stress melts away and I find myself one hundred percent in the moment. It is an exhilarating experience. It's also like a moving meditation, but with a lot of movement: shimmies, hip drops, undulations, box steps, punching, kicking, making figure eights. And, a lot of hollering out of love.

Chatting with a client after class, I have a revelation that if I come into a hard moment, it's harder to access my inner calm if I haven't cultivated that space within myself during a non-stressful time. Deep within this ah-ha moment, I decide to take my light sprinkling of disjointed meditations, and turn them into a practice.

Literally, the next day (funny how life listens sometimes!), I find that a free 21-day guided meditation is being offered online with Deepak Chopra and Oprah. I email Rae to see if she wants to join me in the challenge. Since both of us have attempted to meditate in the past and know how hard it is to make it a habit, we decide to be meditation buddies. If Rae meditates first, she texts me to say she's done (or vice versa). *There is something to be said for accountability.*

Day one. I sit and am soothed by the familiar, soulful voices of Oprah and Deepak. They are the perfect combo to start my morning. I am released from the notions that there is a "right" and "wrong" way to meditate and happily follow along with the guided meditation so that it's not just my mind and me. Really all I have to do is sit, breathe consciously and accept where I am in that moment. I get to let go of my "shoulds" and expectations and just notice where and how the heck I am. If I can just show up and let go, it is really wonderful.

I notice that on some days, I still have a "monkey mind," where my thoughts are going a mile a minute, but they usually slow down if I can just keep coming back to my breath. Most of the time, I connect with myself and notice where I am holding tension in my body. I check-in with how my heart is feeling, whether it is full or contains pieces of emptiness that I need to show up for. I also have times when I actually achieve a blissful state of harmony within my heart, warm and radiating. I cannot expect this, I just have to be happy when it happens. Bottom line: I just need to show up, be still and breathe. Whatever happens in the meditation, I always feel better during and afterwards.

Meditation, like dance, begins to change my life.

# KRAZY KRUSH * MS. DYNAMITE

I go back to the drawing board with Internet dating. *One more try?* Like the last site I was on, this most recent one sends me potential matches via email daily, without my having to do the work of searching. It's also different in that there is a structured system of answering questions before having an email exchange with any potential matches. I appreciate this structure, as it feels a bit like the site acts as needed armor, a turtle shell of protection.

I correspond with Luis. His pictures look cute. His descriptions provide enough detail to get a sense of who he is without over-sharing. He is a lawyer, with an artistic side.

When we progress to chatting on the phone, we have a really nice conversation; yet another chat with a stranger who could be my future partner. *Oh, online dating! Oh, the way my mind works!*

On our first date, we meet at a cafe that specializes in hot chocolate. I am pleasantly surprised by our natural chemistry when I meet him. From his "Hello" with a soft, subtle Spanish accent in a deepish voice, I am intrigued. There is a nice flow of meaningful conversation and subtle flirtation. *This is more like what it should be. Not over the top. Just natural. Easy.*

A few days later, Luis texts to set up the next date for the following weekend. He makes the second date at one of my favorite restaurants (without even knowing it) and we enjoy an amazing meal, even better conversation and more fun flirtation.

"It's so nice to meet you, Heather. After doing some online dating, I seem to always be disappointed by the dates. With you, it feels different. I find myself wondering: Can it really be this easy?" *Is this for real?* I am melting.

The night ends with a lovely kiss that I get lost in.

A few nights later, I head into San Francisco to a hole-in-the-wall, totally charming little restaurant that serves burgers and beer. I chose this place because he had made a comment on our last date about liking fancy restaurants, but also enjoying casual ones.

He arrives before me. As we are seated, the owner remarks, "Oh, I am so glad your girlfriend has arrived." Luis and I both look at each other with a sidewise glance and smile sweetly.

After dinner, we walk to a nearby bar for a drink. I am impressed by his assertiveness while pulling out my chair, ordering my drink without any macho bullshit, which is a hard balance to find in someone. *I really like him.*

As we toast, Luis says, "To new adventures" and then playfully adds with a wink, "with my new girlfriend." We both laugh and talk about how sweet the owner was. Before the night is over, Luis invites me to go to the wine country that weekend. *So exciting!*

Even with a busy work schedule, the few days leading up to our date seem to pass slowly. Finally, Saturday arrives. Luis picks me up, and whisks me away to one of his favorite wineries. Our car ride is a mix of comfortable silence and fun chit-chat. *I am so happy to have met him. Could this be it? Is this what I've been waiting for? Let me just try to stay in the moment and enjoy it.*

We enjoy a bottle of wine on a blanket on the grass. We watch kids play and talk about family, while sharing some meaningful looks.

On the drive back to Oakland, we stop for ice cream, before he drops me back at my house. While I want to invite him up, I also want to wait for anything more intimate, as it's been so long and I want to be sure that we have potential, that there is something there.

I don't hear from him in two days, but then he texts me to say he is sorry he was MIA.

After having dinner the next night, we go back to his house. After kissing for a while, he reaches down to undo my pants. Knowing that I am not ready to sleep with him, I playfully assert, "You don't know me like that yet." With a slight head bob and a smile. We kiss a bit longer and I leave shortly thereafter, as it's getting late.

I text him when I get home to let him know I am home safe and also to thank him. His text reply is, "I had a really great time with you too."

Two days later, I call to inquire about a job interview he had told me he was excited about, and end up leaving a message. That night, he calls, jumping straight into a deeper conversation.

"I almost didn't call you, but I thought it would be worth a shot to share what I am feeling," he begins.

Happy that I have found a man who wants to talk about emotions, yet nervous about what is going on for him, I answer, "Of course."

"I really have been having a good time with you so far. And, I have to say it really hurt my feelings when you pushed back and told me that we did not know each other that well. I actually thought we were progressing and that I do know you pretty well."

"Oh my gosh," I gasp, "I am so sorry! I truly was not trying to make you feel bad at all. I am so glad you told me. From my side, most men are in a way bigger hurry to go further, and I am really looking for something for the bigger picture. Sometimes sex can get in the way of that early on."

Luis' voice softens a bit. "I understand this, Heather. However, your delivery was a bit harsh." *Ouch.*

I have a flashback to the moment and have to giggle internally, as the way it was said was my fiercer side from dance class. "I agree that I was a bit sassy, but I was trying to be playful to lighten the mood of it. It was not intended for it to be hurtful, so I really apologize if that is how it came across. I will also say that I am so glad you called me to talk about this. As I have gotten older, I realize that one of the most important things in relationships in terms of success is to be able to talk about things that come up."

Luis concurs, "Yes, that's why I thought it was worth a call, because I really like you."

"Ahh, I like you too," I reply, happy to be talking with him, thrilled to figure out how to move forward. "Thank you for being so honest and open."

Before getting off the phone, Luis sets a date for the following weekend.

On Friday, however, I receive a text saying that he is under a lot of pressure with the interview process and needs to reschedule our date. I write back immediately wishing him luck and that I look forward to connecting and hearing more about it soon.

I don't hear back. *That's strange.*

At the beginning of the week, I call and leave a message to see how the interview process is going and that I am looking forward to seeing him soon.

Nothing.

As my final attempt a week later, I text, "In my best Lionel Richie singing voice, Hello?" trying to be funny and leave a last offer of humor, just in case he wants to reply.

Nada.

*Crap. I do need someone who can handle my sassy side though.*

# EGO * BEYONCÉ

I am writing in a café, and a man walks in. *Woah. He is attractive. Now, there's some va-va-voom attraction!* I remind myself to focus on my computer.

After a few minutes of pretending to work, I see a woman I'd met a few years prior at a yoga retreat. She sees me through the window, comes in, and excitedly starts talking about wanting to come to one of my dance class. After she leaves, the man looks up and says in a deep voice, as smooth as velvet, "I was not intending on eavesdropping, but I heard you talking about dance."

He introduces himself as Charles. As it turns out, he's a Salsa dancer. I reply that I don't Salsa much perhaps because I have a hard time letting a man lead. *Eeep! Did I really just blurt that?* I immediately follow it with, "Although maybe I have not found the right man to lead me." *Cheesy, but not a bad recovery.*

We somehow end up talking about meditation and the importance of "alternative" health care. He also works in the health world as a chiropractor. He asks me for my number and calls the very next day. In this modern day world of texting, I very much appreciate the old school method of calling.

For our first date, we make plans to have a beverage and watch the sunset. I'm eager to see him again.

Charles shows up looking really sharp. Button-down shirt with the top button undone, shiny shoes, nice jeans that are cleanly pressed. While I am not a huge fan of cologne in general, the scent works on him. It is a really wonderful first date. Flowing conversation, eye contact, and nice physical attraction.

A few days later, we go for a hike. A really lovely second date.

As we continue to hang out over the next couple of weeks. I find myself saying things to my friends that sound really quite hilariously ridiculous. "He is too fit! He works out too much! He calls me too much! He is too fancy! He's like a peacock, tail feathers spread wide to show what he's got!" One of my friends tells me to stop being Goldilocks about this poor man. *It's true, most of the things I am complaining about are things that are actually very important to me in terms of who I am looking for! For goodness sakes, things like being physically fit are on my freakin' list! Do I even know what we want? Is "the list" even relevant?*

I try to figure out why my attraction to Charles is waning. Let me clarify this. Physically, he is very attractive. However, I do not find myself drawn towards him like I did initially. Energetically. Through my massage work and meditations, I have found myself returning to rely more on listening to and trusting my intuition; that little voice that doesn't always make rational sense, but it is very wise. The feelings remind me of other dates when the vibe was off.

I meditate, and when I am done, I take time to reflect. *Is it me? Is it him? Both?* Then, it dawns on me. There is a pattern over the course of our dates of Charles telling a story about a female client.

After our hiking date, Charles shared that he had a client ask him what he had done over the weekend. When he told her that he had gone for a hike, she asked him, "Who were you with?" When he shared that he was with a woman he just started dating, she playfully said, "I hope she's not as beautiful as me!" And he told her, "You are equally as beautiful." If this had been a one-time dealio, then no big deal, but there were always similar stories about women wanting him. My thoughts are either that a) he is very much aware that he was telling me these stories, and is trying to make himself more attractive (which, ironically, had the exact reverse effect) or b) he is not aware, and he has some bigger issues surrounding women and attraction.

When Charles calls the next day, I am writing at a cafe while waiting for my car to get an oil change. I ask him to join me, so that we can both get some work done. *Let's see.*

We hug, and he asks what I am working on. I tell him it is a story about how girls are often given feedback solely on their looks and how this affects their sense of self-worth as they grow up. He nods his head with a deep knowing look. Shortly thereafter, he leans in again, whispering in a seductive voice, "You look so sexy!" I smile back at him, acknowledging to myself that something is not sitting right.

After a few more minutes, he tells me, "I just saw an ex-client walking down the street. She's pregnant now. But, wow, she is still working it! She's still dressing like a Hoochie Mama!" *Oh my God! Who says that?* I give him a look of disbelief, and say, "That's not a very respectful comment." He replies, "Oh, whatever, you know what I mean! Halter top with belly hanging out. Hoochie Mama." *I am done. More than done.* I have left this dating oven on for too long with someone I thought was a gentleman, and I am now feeling charred.

My phone rings and I am saved; my car is ready. I thank him for his offer to drive me, assuring him that I want to walk on my own. While I could say goodbye for real and share the reasons, it has only been a few dates.

After picking up my car, I check with Anna who knows me well. She is very strategic when it comes to challenging or potentially un-comfortable situations. I explain in full detail, and she gives her advice:

Call him (either talk directly or leave a voicemail) saying thank you, but no thank you. THEN, immediately follow this up with a text with the exact same information. This guy is clearly over-testoster-oned and will have a hard time hearing the message, as he thinks that every woman wants him and so this message will be contradicting his truth. By calling and texting, you will be addressing both his auditory and visual learning styles, and he may actually hear the goodbye. *That seems a bit much to me, but it's pretty funny! And, who knows? She might have a point!*

I am hoping for no answer and let out an audible exhale as his voicemail picks up. I then send a text message with a parallel message:

> Hi, Charles. Apologies for leaving you a VM, but I want-ed to let you know that I am not interested in hanging out or moving forward. After reflecting, I do not think we are a match for the bigger picture. Thank you for taking the time to get know me better. I wish you all the best with what you are looking for. Be well.

Two hours later, I get a text in return that reads:

> Actually, I am glad that you picked up on that. I was not sure how to express that to you. Heather you are

a great person too and I am only willing to work on friendship. I can only be friends. Have a great day! Blessings!

Ten minutes later, I receive a phone call with no message. *Strange.*

A week later, I receive a text from Charles wishing me a happy Saturday. *What? I thought this was done!*

Two days later, I get two more calls; the second with a message to call him back. *Nope.*

Four days later, I receive another message from him that he wants to talk about our friendship. *He is not letting up. Seems Anna was right about this one.*

A week after this, I get a message about a potential client he wants to refer to me. *Oh my gosh!* While I debate about whether or not to text back to clarify, I decide that giving any more energy would most likely flame his fire.

Sometimes, people show who they are on the first date, sometimes, the second date; sometimes it takes a few to see some of their true colors. *I need to find a mix of someone who is nice at his core and with whom I have some of the va-va-voom attraction or chemistry element like Charles.*

(Update: A few months later, while on a date, I see him with another woman. He tries to catch my eye, giving me what appears to be a sensual look as he licked his lips, but I looked away quickly, not wanting to engage.)

# I WANNA DANCE WITH SOMEBODY
## WHITNEY HOUSTON

I go on other dates with a couple of men. To be real, they are just more stories. More "it just didn't work out" endings. One was with a nice man with whom the connection was not there. The next was with someone who showed up late for both dates, with no reason or apology. The last was with another peacock, of sorts, who was all about himself. Different details, same results.

I receive another message from the site that lets me know that if I am not getting enough hits, I should consider hiring one of their professional writers to help me with my profile. *Ummm, what? I really depend on people just being themselves by writing their own damn profile.* If there are LOLs after every sentence, I want to know. If you tell me that you believe in casual sex, I want to know. I want to make informed decisions in the weeding out process. Maya Angelou asserts, and I believe wholeheartedly, that people show us who they are, and we need to believe them. *Maybe it's time to jump ship? But, what else will I do? Bars? Clubs? NO!*

A friend informs that she recently got hooked up with a match-making service for free through a friend of hers. While people usually have to pay a pretty steep fee for this "individualized" service, they needed more ladies. She asks me if I was interested in giving it a try. *Why not?*

I am connected via email with Ashlee, the matchmaker. I answer her questions and send a couple of photos. I receive an email back saying that she'd like to introduce me to someone for a one-on-one date. I write back that I'd like to meet with her or at least chat on the phone before committing to anything, so she can get to know me better first. Ashlee calls me, sharing that based on my photos and what I do for a living, I am a good match for many guys. I go on a couple of dates:

A man who has his medical degree but uses it in a non-doctor job. He orders food, although the introductory email parameters clearly state "drinks only." He explains basic anatomy to me, even though I tell him that due to the nature of my work, I know exactly what he is talking about. He's talking to me as if I'm stupid, and he is clearly not listening because he proceeds forward with an Anatomy 101 lesson. He asks if I want to go out again, which is also against the protocol of the service, in which you are supposed to go through the matchmaker. Bye-bye.

A man who is in sales and owns a home in a well-off neighborhood. He is rude to the wait staff, demanding that they make space for us at the bar even though we don't have a reservation. He tells me to repeat myself, as he "didn't hear a thing because I was so distracted by looking into your eyes."

After two dates, I send Ashlee feedback on the guys, saying that they are really not my type at all. She tells me she is really excited about the next one, as he is another sales guy, but also a musician, so he is artistic and practical. We go on a date. He is nice enough, very nervous. There is zero (maybe sub-zero) chemistry. He says he had used this service years ago, and found someone special, but they broke up. So, he returned. He had been doing it this time for around three years, and had not found anyone he liked. But, he really trusted Ashlee.

Just as I am about to email Ashlee to let her know that I am no longer interested in dating through her service, I receive a hasty email that she is leaving the company, and I am welcome to connect with her through her next dating venture, which includes speed dating. The truth is, my "individualized" matchmaking experience was no better than online dating. And, while speed dating is one thing I have not tried, based on how fast-paced my life is already, I say no.

# THAT GOOD GOOD * LEDISI

I . AM. SO. OVER. DATING.

*I just want to meet someone through my everyday life and connections. Is he out there? I think he's out there. I truly feel like I have needed to get comfortable and strong within myself. It's about timing. I feel ready. Maybe, for some reason, he is not ready yet. Will we find each other? And, shit, what is this all about, me wanting to find this partnership? On the one hand, I am a strong, independent happy woman, and on the other hand, it feels like without this person I am somehow incomplete. But, I'm not. What a strange juxtaposition to live within. But, it's real. I am both, I am all. Will I be able to figure out how to be with someone, as I am now so used to being on my own? Should I get a cat? Ahhh! I just need to have faith. I need to focus on what brings me happiness. I need to stop focusing so much on dating.*

I walk up the street to write appreciation letters to friends and enjoy a glass of white wine. It is a beautiful evening.

As I walk in, I am greeted by one of the regular bartenders, who smiles broadly when he sees me. *Hmmm.* When he comes over, he chats to be me about workouts. *Okay, he is not my guy. However, maybe he can be my Mr.-In-The-Meantime-Part-time Lover? It's been so long.* I give him my card.

He doesn't call. I'm not heartbroken by any means, but I am curious and a bit ego-bruised.

The next week, I head back to the restaurant and am greeted by another huge grin. When he comes over, he shares that he put my card by the register, but it had disappeared. I give him another one.

He doesn't call.

*Maybe I am confusing his smile and conversation with my intention? Do I even know what my intention is? While I am on this journey of trying to be my authentic self and find balance in my life, what does it mean that I am thinking about sleeping with this guy? Am I not looking for my Mr. Right? Does my Mr. Right even exist? Where is he? Is Mr. In-The-Meantime okay for now? AND, am I willing to risk giving up my pizza place that I love so much to sleep with him? Oh my gosh, I am losing it!*

I go back one more time, prepared with my intention of needing to find a Mr. Right Now. I order a glass of wine, and try to give him my sexy look. *Too much? I divert my attention back to my phone. Oh. My. God. I am like a crazy person right now. Let it go, Heather.*

He still does not call.

I let it go.

The restaurant ends up closing down a few months later.

After spending so much time trying to invite a distraction, a Mr. Right Now in to my life, I reflect on how much time and energy I spend trying to control and manipulate things to be how I want them to be. Even with all the other good things going on in life, I can lose sight of what is. I forget to live in the present moment. **To be happy with what I already have.** I officially take some time off of dating. I focus on all the love and positivity in my life through friends, danc-ing, massage, family, meditation, reading, and cooking. It's quite re-freshing. I can still feel the pull behind my heart wanting to find my partner, but I also know that I need to come at it from a place of love.

# FREE YOUR MIND * EN VOGUE

A month later, Rae texts to tell me that I should download an app to my phone, as this is the newest way to date. Apparently dating sites are becoming a bit passé. While I have some friends who have tried the app, I know for a fact that it began as a hook-up connection. Rae urges me to try it, telling me that her co-worker used it recently and went on a perfectly normal date.

So, I join.

There are so many people on it. I have to put a restriction of 40 people to say "yes" or "no" to at a time, with a single swipe left or right, determining their fate. Otherwise, I could stay on it easily for a lot longer with all the folk on board. Here's how it goes:

> Nope, no, no, no way, umm maybe (take a pause to look at a few photos, the rest of which are shirtless…so no), no, no, no, please no, oh gosh no, no, no, no, no, no, no, no, maybe (take a pause to read his three sentences including not looking for anything but fun…so no), hells no, no times two.

What I do like about this app is that no one can contact you unless you say "yes."

After teaching a dance class, the studio owner's husband (they met through the Internet), asks about how my dating is going.

"Well, nothing of real interest, but it's entertaining."

"Entertaining?" he seems surprised.

"Let me show you!" I reply and get out my phone to demonstrate. "This is the newest way people find each other. It's not even a website. Just an app. Let's do 40 men together, and I'll let you say yes or no."

I pull up the app, and the first guy that pops up smiles at us.

"Yes or no?" I ask him.

"Wait! How can I decide based on one photo?"

"If you think he's a maybe, let me know, and you can see a few other photos and read a few sentences if he has written anything," I inform him, feeling like I am telling him the rules to a new board game.

"Wow, ok. Well, then, no."

We go back and forth, and he asks to click on a few guys, but a photo or a phrase results in a "no" almost every time. Knowing that I can be very picky, I feel validated in his responses, "Oh my gosh! No! Why does he have his shirt off? Who's that woman with him in the photo? You don't have enough in common. Why didn't he write anything in his profile? He's just a player!" There is one that he says yes to, and when I click "yes," we are a match.

After a week of not getting a message from the guy, knowing that there is literally an entire ocean of women that he can choose from who are playing this game, I delete him and the app.

# ENDLESS LOVE
## DIANA ROSS & LIONEL RICHIE

I go at least once a year to visit to my parents.

We go out to eat at a café. My dad and I both order food. My mom doesn't. Once the food arrives, my dad invites my mom to have some if she wants. She declines. A minute later, my dad loudly taps his plate — TAPTAPTAP — while telling her to help herself yet again. At this point, I remind my dad that she said she was fine. He gives me a look I can't quite read.

A few minutes later, I see my mother grab her fork and take a bite of his chicken.

*What?* While my initial interpretation of the situation was that my dad was not listening to my mom, the truth of it was, he understands her and the dynamics between them, way better than I do.

The entire thing repeats itself again, TAPTAPTAP and all.

What I come to realize more profoundly is that only the two folks involved in a relationship actually know the entirety of it. And, my parents have made it work. Since 1969. In a country in which the stats are up to 50% of marriages ending in divorce, I am intrigued by how <u>any</u> couple can stay together. I ask my mom and dad to tell their story of being married for 46 years, and to share some of their insights on how they have made it work.

Here are their combined words of wisdom:

- Have things you like to do in common and as individuals. Having things we like to do together, like movies or plays or tennis, gives us a common ground on which to connect. At the same time, it is key to have space of our own. This means having your own hobbies and sometimes taking your own separate small adventures.
- Respect each other. All relationships that last are built on this.
- Find ways to communicate. This is going to look different for each couple, but it has to work for the two of you. The good times are good, and there are always challenges that come up. You have to be able to talk about it all.
- Compromise is essential to keeping both people happy. You have to learn to go with the flow, bend a lot on both sides.
- Realize that you both have quirks. It's not so much that you love all the quirks, but that you accept them and work with them.
- You know how to comfort and support each other. It's great when things are good, but how you function when things are rough is even more important.
- That word "l-o-v-e" has something to do with it too.

*I really hope I can find someone who I can have this with.*

When my mom is done sharing, she mentions that she has been praying for a parade for me. "A parade?" I ask, confused. "Yes," she goes on, "I have been envisioning a parade of men for you to choose from." "Mom!" I laugh, "Please stop! I've been watching the parade, and living the parade — I don't want a parade! I just want one person! The right one!" We both laugh.

# GRAVITY * SARA BAREILLES

I dream of reuniting with my First Love. He walks towards me, on his way to find me, and we embrace. We kiss. I am in his arms, and I am safe. Finally. After all these years. I feel tears form behind my closed eyes. I have been waiting for him.

I awake to sadness. And then frustration. *What good is this dream? What does it tell me? How does this help me in my journey? Why am I still having dreams about him?*

It began when I was so young. It was flirtatious and innocent. He was so different than all the boys I knew. Memories of notes on grey lined paper, with his unique cursive writing in black ink, folded up in a special manner, just for me. He asked me questions and encouraged me to find my voice at a time when no one else did. He wanted to know me.

We developed a strong friendship, which continued into high school as penpals. We wrote precious letters back and forth with fierce regularity. Each letter from him was savored, reread countless times, and saved in a special box. For years, we stayed in close touch through this medium, developing a new depth to our relationship as we got to know each other through a free flow of written words. Over time, they also contained sweet confessions of our deeper feelings for one another.

While in college, I was planning on taking a vacation in Spain to visit my family. When I realized that my flight had a planned layover on the East Coast, where he was in school, I was beyond delighted. He was in the midst of finals, and the airport was on the other side of town, but he promised to try his best to make it. I got off the plane, looked around, realizing with great disappointment that he was not there. Sadly, I found a seat, waiting for my transfer.

An hour in to my wait, I looked up to see him walking with great speed down the hallway towards me. I ran to him, and we hugged so intensely, it was if the world ceased. Gravity was defied. People disappeared. Noises faded. Time stood still. The love between us was so deep. So palpable. It was all that existed.

We spent the next hour together, on a cloud in heaven. A first kiss that took my breath away.

We were so enraptured by one another, that my name was called on the intercom to board several times before either of us heard the announcement. Leaving him in the terminal felt as though my heart was literally being ripped out of my chest.

From this meeting, we developed a romantic relationship, seeing each other on any school holiday that afforded us time together. The intensity and love continued to develop. He tended to my heart. He was my sun, my moon, my universe. My heart belonged to him. I would have done anything for him.

I was 23.

I became pregnant.

While it was in neither one of our plans, we decided to have a baby. My life changed. It became about what we were becoming. Love, heart, connection. I realized that there would be challenges, but I wanted them to be with him, to figure it out together. We made plans for him to come to California after he graduated from school to begin our life together.

Three and half months into my pregnancy, everything changed.

Blood. Followed by more blood. Cramps. More blood.

A white ceramic bowl contrasted by crimson red water.

A moment in which I came to realize that I have absolutely no control over the situation. Or, of anything in life.

Rushing out of me, lying in a pool of red, was a tiny baby. A tiny angelic alien is what it appeared to be. The most beautiful and horrific thing that I had ever seen.

It came out of my body.

The sadness pulled my heart down under water and made me feel like I was drowning. It still feels like yesterday. Time alludes events full of profound feeling.

After we lost the baby, he came to visit me, but he quickly backed away from the relationship and moved forward into academia and his future. Without me. He disappeared. He walked away. My heart was shattered for baby and for him, a double loss that was felt beyond numbers or words.

I lost my faith in love.

I lost trust in my body.

It ended.

There was no closure.

This dream is not the first dream he has come into. I usually dismiss them very quickly upon waking. This time, I stay with it. It feels an important piece to my peace. *I have never fully let him go. I need to let him go. The time is now.* The acknowledgment of this feels deeply profound.

# STRENGTH, COURAGE AND WISDOM
## INDIA.ARIE

In addition to this huge ah-ha of realizing that I never let go of My First Love (or, more accurately, the hurt) in order to make space in my heart for someone new, I feel the need to reflect deeply about what I have learned so far. My 39th birthday is approaching. And, while these feel a bit cheesy, here are my authentic love notes to myself:

**Love myself authentically.**
I have to love myself in order to truly and fully love someone else. Taking care of my needs in ways that fulfill me is essential. I need to do things that bring me happiness. I need to treat myself as if I am dating me; do things like blow myself a kiss in the mirror, leave a Post-it love note, buy myself flowers, take myself out to eat. And, be sure to be gentlest on myself during the challenging moments. The only person I need to be is myself. Because I am enough. I get to claim my sexy. Claim my silly. Claim my nerdy. Claim my artistic tendencies. Claim all my 32 flavors and then some!

**Connect with loved ones.**
I have found through life that when you connect with other people, you I better. We are not alone in this journey we call life. It is essential

to share my heart. Vulnerability can lead to deeper connection and understanding. It requires strength and courage to relate to ourselves and to others. Get into conversations that go past the surface into the depths of heart to find deeper understandings. Simultaneously, share laughter with loved ones.

**Move and breathe through challenges.**
Allowing myself to find release in my movements and being brave enough to work through things in the body is so beneficial. This is also true for getting bodywork. Moving the body helps me process my thoughts and feelings when I feel stuck. Breathe. In the hardest moments in life, I oftentimes hold my breath. Breath is life. It's what I can count on as a constant. Exhale and come back to the moment, savor life, repeat.

**Reflect, follow your intuition, and trust the process.**
Reflect on my past and my present. Ask myself, "What am I supposed to be learning from this?" and move forward from this place. Figure out how I am the common denominator in the equation and bring change where needed. Get out of my own way. Go to yoga. Be patient with myself. Trust my intuition. Drop into my heart. Make decisions from this place. Just as a flower needs to emerge from the inside out on its own time, so do I in life. Trust it. Trust myself. History shows I will be okay. The evidence of my life proves it.

# I GOTTA FIND PEACE OF MIND
## LAURYN HILL

Things are as they should be.

It is the eve of my birthday, and I am thrilled to teach two dance classes before heading to Los Angeles to celebrate another trip around the sun. The classes are amazing. My heart is singing. I feel so conscious and grateful to do what I do. I am happy in what I have created in my life. I am in this moment of bliss and peace and love.

Jora picks me up at the airport, and we whirl off to a jazz festival. We drink pink wine, listen to music, and share memories. I am so glad I came.

I receive a phone call with the sad yet somewhat-expected news of the passing of Chantal's dad, Abraham, who was like my second father growing up. Abraham had so much life, so much laughter, so much wisdom. The tears that flow seem to just keep coming, a floodgate opening after being closed for some time.

In talking with my mom, she shares that in her last conversation with him, she told Abraham that he was now in charge of helping Chantal and me figure out our relationships. The thought of him looking down and helping stir the love potion makes me smile through my tears.

The next morning, Jora and I visit the sanctuary my grandfather loved. I know Abraham would have loved it, too. I have a beautiful soulful connection, sending a prayer to both of these important men in my life, and feel their presence. Afterwards, Jora and I go to the beach for a Bloody Mary and cobb salad before taking a nap by the ocean. What a way to bring into my personal new year. What a complex combination of emotions in my heart.

I decide to take a flight back that evening, so that I will have time to take a bath, meditate, and sleep well before driving up to be with family.

At the airport there is no space in my gate so I pull up my Adidas bag, plop down, take a bite of a frozen yogurt, and start to think deeply about life and death. *What happens when we die? Where did you go? We are just energy. The sun, people, everything is just energy. So Abraham turned into pure light, pure love. Why is there so much sadness within me then?*

Lost in thoughts, I suddenly feel propelled to look up. Walking towards me, there he is. My First Love. Who finds me in my dreams. Who no one has compared to. Who I thought I just consciously released. *What? Am I dreaming?*

He walks towards me confidently, knowingly, smiling all the while.

I freeze, unable to move. One hand glued on my spoon in my frozen yogurt.

Suddenly, he is directly in front of me, above me, and I look straight up at him in order to take in his radiance. *You have come back for me. Wait, this cannot be.*

"What the fuck?" I blurt out. No other words will suffice.

Somehow, I manage to rise, slow motion, filled with uncertainty.

*Is this a dream? Is this Abraham's doing?*

He smiles. I remember him. It's the same. *It's you.*

I feel tears well up. He gives me a big bear hug, and I am comforted by the familiarity of his body, the smell of him, and safety that I feel from being pressed against him. *It's you.* It's as though no time has passed.

After our prolonged embrace, we both back up slightly, still standing close with what feels like a magnetic pull between us. Eyes connected. Hearts syncing. It's all that exists.

I shake my head side to side, as if attempting to wake myself if it is a dream. *I let you go. I un-invited you from visiting me in my dreams so I can go on with my life and find new love. What are you doing here?*

As if reading my mind, he shakes his head knowingly.

"This is crazy," I finally share out loud.

He smiles at me again, the corner of his mouth slightly turned up, not dropping eye contact. *I know you. I love you. You came back for me. You are the end to my love story. My First Love.*

It is as if he can see into my soul. Like he always could. He sees me.

It is me that finally has to look away. Some part of my brain tries to remind me that he is married with two small kids, but I quickly dismiss this Facebook knowledge.

When he inquires about why I am in L.A., I tell him Abraham's passed away and I am going back to be with my family. He offers his condolences and shares, in eerie coincidence, that he is coming from a funeral. We talk for a few moments about death. The vulnerability of life. About cancer. About what happens when we die. Why those of us that are left are so sad.

In the midst of this depth, I am jolted by a thought that is blurted out, "Why are you going to Oakland?"

"I just moved to Oakland."

*Just you? We get to be together? You've finally come back for me? You are my happy ending?*

"Why?" I can feel some hardness coming through in my sudden speculation.

"For work. I was in Seattle, finishing my internship. Then, I was in Arizona, teaching." He starts to tell me about his success within his profession, which I don't care to hear. He was always in school, always studying, always enhancing himself, which I saw through as he never felt like he'd done enough, achieved enough. But, he was enough. He had always been enough.

I become keenly aware of my body language, which shows discomfort. I rock side to side a bit, cross and uncross my arms. I feel awkward in my body. *What if you aren't here for me?*

"How are you?" he asks.

"I am well," I assure him. *Is this true? Yes. I am happy. Minus the desire to be in a relationship and the present heartbreak of Abraham's death. But, everything else is good. I have found happiness and peace. I just want to find Love. Wait! IT'S YOU!*

I interrupt my own thoughts to express, "You've just caught me in a hardish moment. Death is crazy and brings up so much. And, I am so thrown by this. By you. Really, how can this be? What are you doing here?"

I shake my head again and look away. I look back to find him still looking at me, no fear, maybe a little sadness.

"You were just in my dream," it comes out in vulnerable whisper. Trying to downplay it, I don't mention that he is in so many of my dreams.

"You are in my dreams too." He understands.

I can feel my ribs expand as I inhale swiftly in order to exhale in knowingness. *Of course.*

He asks me to sit with him on the ride up. We board, making our way to the back of the plane where there are many seats. A woman in front of me stops suddenly, causing him to bump up against me from behind. I can feel his body. His breath. The past memories merge with this present reality of him. *I want to melt into you.* We both mutter "sorry" at the same time. *Please come closer. Never let me go.*

We sit side by side. There is an undeniable fire. A fire from age fourteen. The same fire that happened in our meeting in another airport in college. The fire that led me to fall in love, become pregnant, to be soul connected to the point that I have still have dreams about him all these years later. The same fire I had that led me to have a dream, all those years ago, of his mother dressed in white, sitting on a bench so calmingly, knowingly, peacefully only to find out the next morning that she had died that night. Our fire, our connection, runs deep.

Our eyes meet without breaking away until I glance down at the gold ring on his finger. *I shouldn't be looking at him this way.* It is not sexual, it is not romantic. It is soul. It is beyond words.

After he shares that he knew that we were going to run into each other, he proposes that we be back in each other's lives. I internally shake my head, wondering where the hell my deep groundedness from meditation is in this moment. There must be a reason this is happening. Am I supposed to have some great epiphany in which I am released like the trapped bird inside my heart being set free?

I share with him, "I have dreams of you, more than just the one. I wake up angry."

"I have dreams of you too," he says softly, "I am sorry that yours make you angry."

I feel flustered by these words, "Maybe angry is not the right word, but I wake up not knowing why you are there, and that makes me frustrated."

"That's fascinating," he connects to the strong emotion, but in his own way, "I used to wake up sad. Now, when I dream of you, I wake up and am not surprised anymore. The dreams have become normal. They make me smile."

He is not supposed to say such things to me. For over a decade, I have put him in the deepest chamber of my heart so as to stay protected. He only exists there. It has been so long that I thought that he must have forgotten about me and it was my job to keep our connection sacred and safely tucked away. *Sacred is the word to describe what we shared.*

As the flight takes off, sunlight hits his eyes, making them translucent. I can see his thigh, his chest, his profile. *I know every inch of you.*

"What happened?" I quietly ask, from the deepest place in my heart. A place that embodies both the hardest and softest of my vulnerability.

He shares with me about his process of dealing with death, confusion, loss, and depression. At the end, he asserts, "You've asked me this before."

"I know," I say remembering our conversation a decade ago. "But it still does not make sense to me."

There is pause. I turn to him again, "You know, while it's neither here nor there, I would have been there for you."

"I know, Heather. I did not feel left by you."

I turn away, my mind screaming "BECAUSE YOU LEFT ME." This is where my anger and frustration collide upon waking. I do not share in this moment.

*Why are we here? Why are you married? Are you married? Why am I not in your life?*

"Heather, we were so young. There was just so much loss."

The loss of his mother to cancer when he and I were together, followed directly by the loss of our child. We could not find each other through it. I lost my sense of purpose.

Breaking me from my painful reminiscence, he shares again, "I have been thinking about running in to you. I knew it would happen. I wasn't planning on it being in LA, though." *Well, at least you knew. I had no fucking idea. Where is my Zen side now?* I keep looking away, notice that I am breathing too shallowly and take a huge inhale.

I wonder if maybe this was supposed to happen so that I can have closure and can move on. Fully. Only, my feelings for him, my love for him, my desire for him, somehow feel the same, as if it is merely a few days that have passed instead of all these years.

We go back to talking about safer things. We fill each other in our career endeavors. He tells me he has so much going on that he put his underwear on backwards the day before. My loud laughter in response to this reminds me of who I am now. Happy, unreserved, full of heart. *Breathe.*

He tells me again that he wants me in his life, although he's uncertain of what that may look like. He'd been having this conversation in his head for when we finally met. *He really wants me in his life. I want that too. So much. Too much.*

I tell him again that I don't know.

"I have to be honest with how I am feeling."

"That's all you've ever been with me," he says in a voice that is like silk caressing my skin. *Funny, because I can't always find the words to express how I am feeling with other men in my life.*

I explain to him that at this point of unexpected connection, I simply, or rather complicatedly, don't know. That he has not been in my life for over a decade except in my dreams. That after he wrote to tell me he was engaged and moving to Seattle and asked about my brother, I wrote back wishing him the most support I could muster and he never wrote back. He literally wrote me off. Again. I learned to live without him. I tell him that while I have been in relationships, I am still searching for my one. I share that it is only recently that I discovered that it comes back to him time and time again. I tell him that I still don't understand, that it's where I have a stuck point in my life. I tell him that I am looking for someone who can look at me the way he did, with eyes that somehow see my soul. And, because he still looks at me this way, I don't think I can be in his life at this point.

"Heather, we are only halfway through our lives and we are going to keep meeting."

I have a flashback of our bodies connected, sharing the infinite universe. *I wonder if you can read my mind, if this is cheating.*

My eyes return to the gold around his finger. *I cannot do this to her. To me. I was supposed to be her.*

I keep shaking my head in disbelief. *How is this possible? Am I about to wake up wondering if this really happened?*

The pilot announces we are descending. It has gone too fast. *How is time still moving? Shouldn't the world stop to acknowledge this? Is this Abraham at work?*

I am not ready to let him go.

I drive him to his home. To his house. With his family, although we have not spoken of them.

He asks for a way to contact me. I give him my email, but tell him I don't know. He says we can start there. *Start? What does that mean?* I cannot give him my number, as I cannot have him call me. I cannot talk to him. I cannot have this magnetic pull back in my life. He sends an email from his phone, making sure that it goes through, as if not having the option to connect would break his heart.

I get out of the car to hug him. We are so close. We still fit. It's just like I remember. It's just like in my dreams. I look at him, wanting for things to be lighter and say, "Well, it's been surreal."

I watch him for a moment as he ascends the stairs to his home. I drive away before he opens his door. I cannot.

The tears that flood from my eyes are many. I can barely see as I drive, but I cannot stop.

My emotions crashing in and exploding out, I text Rae to see if I can stop by. I do not know what to do with myself. I am elated and exhausted and confused. I am everything and nothing.

Rae does not reply. I call her. No answer. I drive over. I cannot be with just myself. I cannot handle this. I don't know what to do.

Rae opens the door, and my words make no sense, slurred and loud, "I was eating Pinkberry frozen yogurt. And, he is there. And, I can't. I just can't..."

I see Rae's husband slowly get up and make his way out of the room, as she hugs me and I spontaneously collapse onto the floor. She listens as I spew. By the end of my story, I am flailing. "I just don't understand. This makes no sense to me. I would get it if I saw him and did not feel this way, if I could understand that it was time to let him go because we changed and to have closure, but the feeling is still there. I don't understand."

Rae offers, "I know it does not make sense, but with all things in life, as you have learned, it doesn't always make sense in the moment. But, it clearly was meant to be. I think this will help you find resolution, in some way, even though we don't know what that looks like right now."

Realizing that I will not have any answers, and also feeling a heavy tiredness within my body, my shoulders slump forward and I tell her, "I was coming home early so that I could take a bath, meditate, go to bed early to be ready to be around family for this death. I was on a flight that I was not supposed to be on."

I leave with uncertainty, yet also with a quiet strength inside me.

As I drive home, exhausted, I call Chantal. I talk with her every day since Abraham's passing. I also can't help but share with her the state that I am in. Today is no different. I have to let go of the guilt I feel about adding this on to her grief.

I find myself parked in front of my house, keys in my lap, lights still on, hunched forward, sobbing between words on the phone with her.

In a moment's time, I sense something is not right. I sit up, look to my left to see two men standing on the opposite corner. My gut tells me I need to get out of here. "One second," I tell my friend, "I just need to move my car." Since I am parallel parked, I have to back up before pulling out of the spot I have been in. When I look up, while putting my car in drive, I see one man coming directly towards me. I can see him reach into his jacket. "Hey!" he yells, with his eyebrows furled, while aggressively motioning to roll down my window. *Fuck.*

"What's going on?" Chantal asks, a hint of panic in her voice.

"Hold on, Love," I say, surprised by the external calm that does not match the fear and adrenaline that is making me breathe quickly. You never know how you will react in situations like this.

My neighbor had just told me that his wife had been mugged on our street the month prior. At knifepoint.

I realize within a split second that I may hit him as he comes closer and I pull out. *Whatever you have planned is not going to happen, mother fucker. You are not going to take anything from me. And, I am not going to live with fear. There will be no more of an exchange here.* I do not hesitate. I refuse to back down and feel threatened. *If it's gonna be between me or you, it's <u>not</u> gonna be me. I do not believe in violence, but in this situation, you cannot hurt me. I will run you over if I need to.* I skim by, barely missing hitting him. The look in his eyes is hard and cold. I stare directly in his eyes, without hesitation, without fear, with a don't-fuck-with-me attitude.

I fly through the stop sign, passing his partner on the corner.

"What's going on?" my friend inquires, growing worry evident in her voice.

"It's okay. Hold on, Love. I just need to be sure I am away." I do not want to disturb her more.

I come to the stoplight, a few cars in front of me. I wish they were not there, so I could run through the light and get some distance. But, it's okay, because there are other cars. I am safe.

Then, I look in my rearview mirror. Both men have crossed the street and are walking down the narrow divider towards me. I see what appears to be a shiny object in the main guy's hand. They are getting closer.

FUCK! I just need the light to turn green. *Just think green.*

I brace myself, then exhale, and have faith.

The light turns green. I go.

I tell my friend what happened. She wants me to call the police, but all I want to do is take my bath. I drive around for a while, talking with my friend, reeling at this day. The last few days. A 39th birthday. A death. A trip. An unexpected encounter. A near carjacking.

When I am sure the coast is clear, I make my way back to my apartment, parking in a different spot than usual, and cautiously and quickly go inside. To my bath. *What the fuck just happened?*

# NEXT LIFETIME * ERYKAH BADU

I wake up to an email from My First Love, an empty subject line, but pregnant in content. He's amazed at the synchronicity of our meeting. Wondering how I am. *I cannot.*

I drive up north to my family. Celebrate life, mourn loss. I do not understand life in this moment, but know that it will work out and I have things to learn.

I drive back home, somehow not afraid for my safety. Feeling strong and vulnerable all at once.

I do not want any of it to be stuck in my body, as things from the past had been. I book a massage and a therapy appointment.

I have dance classes scheduled the next day, and while I know that I am not going to be able to show up in my usual energetic way, it is a part of my process. I briefly tell the class what I have been through and, as tears form, we begin to dance. I cannot look at myself. The ladies join me in my therapy, perhaps tapping in to their stories, differing in detail from mine, but somehow unifying our movement and our hearts. I am thankful for them allowing me to move through this in a way that is deeper and difficult.

The next day, I arrive for my massage, appreciative to have had a relationship with my massage therapist for years. I cry through my entire session. She finds all the places in my body that I have had to hold on to, feeling truly as if there is armor surrounding me. I share with her through tears that in the past, had any one of these things happened, I would have taken it in without feeling it fully. Then, it would have been incorporated into my hardness, my protective shell, my wall to the world. With the weight of all these stories coinciding, I have no choice but to break open, feel fully. I cannot compartmentalize and put them away for another day. It's just too much. **Rather than harden, I want to breathe into these experiences, let go of what doesn't serve me, and soften into my heart. Open my heart to the sky and embrace the strength in vulnerability.**

At therapy two days later, I find words to express myself. The stuck-ness to him and around him is still there. He's back and I don't want to let him go.

I email him, sharing my experiences.

We write back and forth a few times, it's sort of a blue and black poetry, that of the night sky and the deepest part of the ocean. Charged with emotion and connection between us.

As my therapist points out, this is how we have communicated our whole lives, and that instead of poetry, I need to be straightforward, take charge, and ask him where he is at with his marriage.

While I initially resist this, I know she is right, as the poetry we speak to each other is made of the past. So, I ask. Only to be met with an email that baffles me. While he starts by stating the amount of time he has been married, it is followed by, "I am curious as to why you ask," and then, "If this had been a few years ago, she (and I) would have wondered about this (re)connection and it's unclear motives, but now that we are in a place of everyday life with kids and jobs, this is no longer true."

*He's trying to downplay the fire and minimize what we both felt. That is bullshit.* While I do not want to say goodbye, I know that I have to.

I revisit the email that I wrote the night we reunited, clearly knowing that it was going to eventually be goodbye. But, we have to be ready for such things. It's not done until you are ready to be done. My mind attempts to play tricks on me like it did with my Ex, the place where you can go in your brain to the fantasy. However, my fantasy of him returning to me has tripped over the reality of the situation. He did not choose me. I do not choose him.

So, I write an email entitled, "It's All."

Dearest,

I have had to take some time to ground myself with all the areas that life has opened up recently in the most profound of ways. As I previously expressed, I have also needed time to sort out where I stand in regards to you. Still my reaction is: Wow. Just wow. And, while I acknowledge that this is still coming from a place of complete rawness and vulnerability, I need to express my heart from this place. To you.

Here is my flow to share:

This past Spring, I had the (surprising) realization that I had not let you go. While I had done many things to let you go, through writing, other relationships, conversations, and dancing, you still appeared to me in my dreams. Countless times. I would let you drift away quickly upon waking, after feeling angry at the reality of waking without you there, and then annoyed that you somehow were still in my dreams after all this time. It wasn't until a few months ago that I truly acknowledged the significance of you still being there; the reality that somewhere in my deepest place in my soul, you still resided in my heart. Seems crazy due to the time-frame being well over a decade ago. Through conscious reflection, I realized that from my side, one of the reasons it did not work between us at that time was because I was coming from a place of need, of desperation, of feeling broken, and incomplete, and wanting you to fill this.

From a tender age, you somehow saw me completely, the essence of me. You asked questions from a genuine place and asked me to express myself at a time in my life when I did not believe in myself, and you did. I felt loved by you, fully. It was unique, true, and life-changing. I felt and still feel so grateful, so honored, for the energy, curiosity, passion, truth, completeness, abandon, confidence, and presence that you shared with me. You have helped shaped me into the woman, the person, that I have become.

You were the first man that I have completely loved. You are the only man that I have loved with no hesitation, no pauses, no holding back.

This love, for me, was unbreakable. Stronger than a million suns. Beyond words. Beyond age. Beyond time.

Looking back on old emails, I am not sure that I accurately expressed the entirety of this depth of my desire after our separation. I do recall you telling me in a conversation that you were not my sun. I remember my devastation upon hearing these words. To me, you were. You were my everything. In the few years to follow, I tried my best to be real, yet somehow cool, in our correspondence. I felt that any connection with you was better than none. I think you knew/know from our meetings that there has always been so much more.

I cannot begin to understand the journey and process you underwent in the time we have not been together, because I have not really been a part of it. To me, the reality is that after we lost our baby all those years ago, you stepped away from me in a huge way, a significant way, a way that has haunted me. The random dots since that time occurred led to a complete and total silence of nearly a decade after you told me you were engaged. Eight years is a long time. And while you could argue that I said that this love is beyond time; to put into measure and perspective: a mere day without you has been a long time.

I cannot fathom how the reality of you has not resurfaced earlier into my world after all this time, until now. Especially in this fashion. With these circumstances, and (from my perspective) these restrictions.

I have learned to live without you.

Not because I wanted to, but because I had to.

Then, we meet. After all this time. By chance, because of God, maybe our ancestors doing, perhaps due to the Universe conspiring for it to happen, undeniably from the gravitational pull between the moon and the waves that parallel us.

For me, this journey I have been on has been vast and amazing. I've learned self-awareness, love, and healing that I would not have learned otherwise. So, I am thankful and appreciative. Deeply. But, also sad that it has been without you. Perhaps that is the sense you have from your dreams. I am certain that we both have life stories that could be shared for hours and hours: a lifetime of connection that would allow both of us to feel met, heard, and understood in ways that could only exist between us. I know this, because the looks between us, even though the details are different...the looks are still the same.

I do not know what you meant initially when you said that you want me to be in your life. I have ruminated on this, tried to make sense of it, what this would look like, what it would feel like. As I said on our flight, I have not found someone else with whom to share the energy that exists between us, or anything close. It sounds like you have, even though it must be different. Any which way, that puts us, you and I, in very different positions at this particular point in time. You see, what I understand radically, with every cell in my being, is that when we looked at each other, even though it was unexpected in every way, I still see the Universe. I see infinite love. I see beauty. I feel depth beyond words. I see understanding. Pain that wants to be healed. Souls that want to unite.

None of which I can hold.

My inclination is to kiss the essence of you. To inhale your breath with mine & marvel in their intertwining, the beauty, the struggle, the positive, the challenge, and all the spaces that lay in between. I want to look into your eyes every day I am still breathing. I want any piece of you that I can hold. I want. I want. I want. Surely, this offer of being in each other's lives, as pen-pals or friends, is better than nothing? Better than emptiness. Silence. Wondering. Void. Being without. Better than glimpses of connectedness that exist only in dreams?

Then, I come back to the color of the ring on your finger. Gold. Screaming. My confession to you, to myself, is that, crazily enough, after all this time that has passed, I have wanted it to be me. This is perhaps the question that I have been truly trying to ask you these past few times that we have had the chance to look into each other's eyes. It's not "What happened?" Rather, it's: "Why didn't you come back to me? To us." I still had not given up hope. Since so recently figuring this question out, I have meditated, and reflected deeply. I do not know the answer. I also have come (initially and hesitantly) to profoundly understand that I do not need to know the answer. **It's All.** It is what it is. I breathe in to this, with the aim of accepting. At this moment, my accepting means something different than what you have expressed and have seemingly imagined for us.

I have to let you go. My dear heart. My sweet love.

Perhaps we will meet next lifetime to try again, to honor the fire in our eyes & the depths of our soul connection that is like every flower on this earth & heaven combined. Now that I am letting you go, maybe my lifetime partner will show up. Then maybe we can be friends.

But, I am beyond certain that at this point in my existence that I cannot look at you without wanting more.

Which is not fair to the people in the life that you created.

So, I thank you. I thank you endlessly, with echoes of forever, for the initial, pure, complete love you brought into my life. We, indeed, helped shape each other as we have grown. This innocent love, my sweet love, will remain. Always. I have no doubts that we will continue to whisper and shape one another in ways that run deep, internally, in lines with our bones, our spirits, our very essence. In ways that are profoundly connected, like I am to my grandfather and you are to your mother...in ways that do not require everyday reality, but exist without a doubt, with infinite love that is beyond being grasped.

And, I wish you the best in the journey you are on. Truly. Because that's what you do for love. You set it free. I set "us" free.

The heartache, the holding on, the waiting, the wanting more, the dreams of past in my present; I release...

I let go.

With tears...

With uncertainty...

With pieces of peace...

With faith that all will be as it should...

And, somehow, with this (re)connection...

With a deeper faith in love.

It's close to midnight. And, I press send. I am so tired.

Without having given thought to what comes after, just knowing that it must be done.

I sit.

Expressing my vulnerability without needing a response.

I am feeling simultaneously empty and full.

*Shit! Wait! Will he write me back? Is that it? Am I done?*

There is no wave of relief. But, I am still breathing.

I go to bed.

I wake up to an email from him that says he's blown away by my words. He loves me, has always loved me. He needs time to respond further in order for us to find our new path.

My final therapy appointment is two hours later. I receive the advice that I need to choose what to do next. I can block him so that I don't hear about his process. Or, I can receive his messages and will have to make the choice to write back or not.

Before I consciously decide, I receive another email from him, this one parallels the length, intensity and reflection of mine.

I receive them — words that soothe my soul.

I do not reply.

# I USED TO LOVE HIM * LAURYN HILL

A week later, I meet with my friend Yasmina to see a movie. I see her from across the street, with a frown on her face. *That's strange. I hope she is okay.* I cross the street, beaming a smile, waving heartily.

As I get closer, I realize that she really does not look happy. Just as I take a step up onto the curb, I glance to the right. My Ex. Talking with a woman.

Yasmina looks at me, grabbing my elbow, and takes a sharp left to walk down the street with me.

"What the eff is happening with all these exes?!" I ask her in disbelief.

"Seriously," she replies. Then, she goes on to tell me that he tried to make eye contact and say hi to her, but she just turned the other direction.

Later that night, I take some time to figure out what message the Universe is trying to tell me. I call Yesenia, and tell her that while I don't understand, I was happy that I did not have a huge emotional charge around it. I also mention to her that he really was the best boyfriend in all aspects of our actual relationship (except, of course, the cheating).

"Well, that's huge, Heather. I have not heard you say that since the end of your relationship," Yesenia says.

"So true! And, I spent so many years feeling convinced that if/when I ever saw him, I would yell and spew anger at him. This time, while I had no desire to talk with him, I felt a moment of sadness for what was and then an appreciation for the good times we shared."

Life is pushing me to deal with the past. Reflection, letting go and heart healing have all risen on the path to greet me.

# STRONG AS GLASS * GOAPELE

Life continues to move forward.

In the midst of the craziness and despite not feeling quite ready, I decide to take the leap into teaching massage.

I am exhausted, but my heart is so open.

While I teach technique, I realize that my emphasis is on self-care, intuition, communication, connections, and listening deeply. I am challenged, humbled, and honored. I grow stronger and am grateful. So grateful for trying something new even though I am terrified. In the past, being afraid put my life on hold. Now, I consciously choose to face my fear, explore it, and allow it to propel me through rather than stop me from trying. Fear no longer holds me captive, rather, it pushes me to act. It becomes a catalyst for moving me forward. There is still vulnerability that exists within this process, and in this vulnerability, there is also strength. **Vulnerability is strength.**

On my way up to Abraham's memorial service, I receive a third email from My First Love, wanting to make sure I received the other two. I weigh whether or not to answer, and I decide that we both need closure. I write back to him, letting him know that I did receive his emails, thank him for the unexpected peace they brought me, and conclude that while fate brought us together, it is my conclusion that it is time to say good-bye.

I also realize that I now embody many of the practices and ways of being I admired and appreciated about him for years: meditation, spirituality, authentic self, having deeper conversations. I am also no longer coming from a place of need, or desperation, of feeling broken and incomplete, and in need of someone else to fix it, or fill me. I have become my own well of love.

# READY FOR LOVE * INDIA.ARIE

A few nights later, I dream of my Ex. We are on a bike. He is in the front, carrying me on the back, pedaling hard up a hill. I am thinking there is no way he is strong enough. And, yet, up we go.

*Why do I keep having dreams with past loves?* I choose to journal and am amazed at the insight I find. I feel like dreams tap in to my unconscious. When I look at dreams that have other people in them, I interpret their presence as a symbol of a particular part of myself. To me, my Ex has represented broken parts of me that were not attended to. The weakest, most vulnerable parts. While my initial thought in this dream is he (I) can't make it up this hill, he (I) is/am stronger than I realize.

I am reminded of an article I read once about butterflies. Scientists noticed that caterpillars spent a disproportionate amount of time in their cocoons compared to their time as butterflies. Trying to be helpful, they prick the cocoons so that the butterflies could emerge earlier than they would have naturally, in order for them to spend more time in the outside world, flying and being free. What they discovered, however, was that when the butterflies were taken out early, they could not fly. Their wings were not strong enough because they hadn't gone through full metamorphosis and transformation within the cocoon. The time spent in the womb is a part of the readiness, and it cannot be rushed. It is part of the process towards becoming.

Becoming is messy.

Complicated.

It can be painful.

Beautiful.

Hopeful.

Non-linear.

A continual movement, a dance.

It's about embracing our hardness appropriately, while simultaneously finding ways to soften.

Seeking ways to feed our souls, especially in the challenging moments.

Letting go of the shit that does not serve.

Breathing.

Showing up for the process.

Time and time and time again.

Reaching for the truth within our hearts.

Relishing connections along the way.

Having faith.

Trusting the flower to bloom in its own time.

It has taken my whole life to arrive at this moment.

While I am certain there will continue to be moments of both tears and laughter in this beautiful struggle, history (herstory) shows that I will be all right. And, sometimes, I'll be fucking fabulous.

I am ready.

I am.

**Ready**.

# EPILOGUE:
## MY MOM'S TALE OF MEETING MY DAD

Reflecting upon my dating herstory, it sparks curiosity about my mom and dad's story. The entirety. I ask my mom to share with me, knowing that what I was exposed to is probably a huge part of how I view what it means to be in love and in a committed relationship.

From my mama, with a whole lot of love, and a little sass in the mix:

> School had already started on a military base in Kenitra, Morocco in August 1967, when I moved there as a new teacher. I was settled into my room in the "Kenitra Hilton," part of the Bachelor Officers Quarters system: two very basic rooms with a connecting bath. The teachers there taught at either the elementary school or the high school, and ate together at the Officers' Mess.
>
> Jane was a tall, attractive, forward and annoying twenty-something teacher who announced that another new teacher was on his way. She had somehow conned someone in the high school office into looking

at his file. She shared that he was in his thirties and short. His name was Fred. She was clearly disappointed with this information, as he obviously did not fit her qualifications as an eligible man.

In a week, the gentleman himself showed up in the Officers' Mess. He was tired. He was discouraged. He had been sent to Italy first, only to find out that they had no job for him. But, there had been an opening in Morocco, so they sent him there instead. As he had resigned from his job in Illinois and sold or stored all of his possessions, he decided to take the job. My first response to this man who was bent over his food across from me was pity, which I expressed to him as he sat morosely eating his lunch.

It was a small base and we (teachers) were an even smaller group. As such, we often did things together. We traveled a lot. I particularly remember the time a group of us went on an overnight trip to a beach resort in Skhirat. One of the King's palaces was nearby so there were a lot of Moroccan soldiers on the beach. I was not generally aware of body builds, but when we all appeared in our swimsuits, I became aware of a tan, muscular body. I was impressed. It was Fred. (I bought my first workout outfit once we started dating.) He wore a gold chain around his neck with a gold disc which had on it "Never feel sorry." I was a bit concerned about that, but, I found out it he had wanted it to say "for yourself," but it did not fit on the pendant.

At this time, I was dating a nice, young lieutenant. Fred dated one of my friends, Gabriela, though not seriously. It did not pan out for me with the lieutenant, and I was very sad about it and decided to transfer out to Norway three months later.

One night, during my last few months in Morocco, another friend, Ellen, invited both Fred and me to go to the Feast of the Throne in downtown Kenitra. This was a celebration to honor the King of Morocco. The three of us drove in Ellen's M.G. which was quite a feat as it had only two seats. We arrived at the dusty downtown area which was now a tent city. We parked the car, paid the car guard, and began walking and gawking at all the activity. We had not gone far when some men came out of one of the tents and invited us inside. I have no idea why they did that, but it was very intriguing.

They were dressed in white robes which probably meant they had made the Hajj to Mecca. We sat on the rugs and pillows and drank quarts of sweet, delicious mint tea and more than our share of cookies. And we were entertained! There was a television going on, connected to an outlet somewhere by a long and dusty cord. There were comedians playing out the time-honored, many-culture story of a country bumpkin who comes into town and meets two sharp city boys. There was also a man who was singing a lament about his wife who had left. The crowd was cheering and laughing, and opining that he was much better off without the wife...no sympathy for him at all. We enjoyed ourselves for a very long time, and were not sure when best to make our exit. Finally, the volume of tea hitting our bladders emboldened us to thank our hosts and leave. We found our car, crammed ourselves in, and returned to the Hilton. After I found out he was not dating Gabriela, I invited Fred in for a drink. And we talked, and talked. We found that we were both interested in history and classical music. We traded family stories. We talked in to the wee hours. And that was the beginning. He asked me out for another night.

I told my friend who had been casually dating Fred that he had asked me out, and asked if it was okay. (What was she going to say?) So, with her permission, we began dating. We went to plays at the small local theater, out to Mama's, a wonderful restaurant on the beach nearby that specialized in mussels and garlic, lamb brochettes and the best flan ever created.

Dating anyone on such a small base was awkward. My next door neighbor, Anne, an older teacher, warned me about Fred. "You don't want him!" she told me. She was sure he had married before. I asked her how she knew, and she told me she just knew about things like that. Everyone knew everyone's business.

Besides our fun outings, Fred and I were also in the habit of having paper-grading dates, a tradition that lasted throughout our lifetime which has now morphed into "library dates." He held my hand in public, not caring who saw. We kept dating: March, April, May.....I had already put in for a transfer to Norway at the beginning of the semester, and of course, just as we were getting closer, it came through. More awkwardness. Should I ask if he wanted me to turn down the transfer and stay to be with him? He did not ask me to stay, so I decided not to push it. The movers came to pack up my belongings. And, I packed to go home to California for the summer to visit family before heading to Norway. "Well, that's that," I thought.

Relationships so far had not worked out for one reason or another. Why should this one be different?

Wonder of wonders, when I got to California, I got a letter from Fred. He was coming from Chicago to see me....driving a car for someone...delivering it to Hollywood. He met my family for the first time. They were not impressed - something they did not let on (wisely, I suppose) until much later after we were married and they had gotten to know him. He used the defense he had used with his own family in Chicago, which was when he felt ill-at-ease, he would read (hide) behind a newspaper rather than have conversations.

After a couple of weeks, he returned to Morocco, and I got ready to go to my new assignment in Norway. Again, as we had not made any commitments, I thought, "Well, that's that!"

Again, I was surprised. Letters arrived in Norway as I settled in. They continued steadily in very organized weekly intervals. Prosaic in style, but always with a nice thought at the end. We made plans to meet at Christmas, and again at Easter. Fred decided to go to Nevada to work on a Master's degree, so he was packed and prepared to leave the system.

We met in Morocco. I had resigned from my job in Norway, in hope that he might suggest some permanency to our relationship. But, I had a backup plan. My cousin and her husband were moving to England. I planned to go see them and perhaps pick up a job on the American base there.

On the last day of our time together in Morocco, I tried to express my feelings. His response: He was afraid of a committed relationship after watching some of the marriages of friends and family, many of which were not happy. Then...in his chair, he fell asleep. (I think this was a variation of the newspaper ploy). So, I saw him off at the Casablanca airport tearfully, and gave him a letter to take with him to express my thoughts. But as the plane took off, I thought again: "Well, that's that."

I was sad and somewhat disgusted. I wondered what was wrong with me. I made up my mind that I would stop looking. I was fine on my own. Two friends arrived in Morocco, and we drove from Morocco through Spain and up through Europe on an adventure of our own. We drove to Germany, let one friend off, and then my friend Kristen and I drove to England. Kristen's aunt and cousin invited us to stay in Sussex, England, where we had a wonderful time, and filled our days exploring and making brass rubbings in churches. We both went to Cambridge when my cousins arrived and stayed with them awhile.

At their home, waiting for me, was a stack of letters from Fred. I arranged them by date and began to read. They were mostly the prosaic accounts of how his days were organized and the classes he was taking. About four letters down was a letter with a proposal. Surprise, surprise!

I wrote back, accepting, and I arranged for my return ticket. Kristen, kindly drove my Volkswagen back to Holland for shipping to New Jersey. I had to coordinate the plane ride with the arrival of the car. It was not an easy trip. I had three matching Samsonite suitcases crammed with souvenirs and possessions, which I somehow managed to get on a bus to Bayonne, New Jersey, where the car was, but I made it. I then began an odyssey, making my way slowly to my fiancé. I still harbored a tad of resentment from the discussion we had had before he left, so I decided to visit everyone I knew starting with the East Coast. I drove as far as Connecticut, then started across country alone. It took two months. It was one of those things that in hindsight I would probably never do again, but when you are young, wise moves are often in short supply. I made it all the way across, to where he was in Reno, Nevada. We made plans for a wedding about four weeks away at Christmas, on the anniversary of my brother's first marriage and the anniversary of my cousin Betty's marriage.

My mother made all the dresses and was sewing up hems until the day of the wedding. I borrowed my cousin Betty's handmade wedding dress. My mother kept saying, "Please go to Las Vegas. Elope!" but my father was determined to have a wedding for us. The wedding was lovely. We were married in the Santa Anita Church in the middle of a sandstorm. My cousin Roberta, my sister-in-law Mary, and my cousin Betty all agreed to be bridesmaids on short notice. Fred corralled my brother, his brother, and a cousin to be groomsmen. It was a beautiful service. The sweat of his hand went through my glove.

We drove from California to Nevada to begin our life together, via Carmel for a short honeymoon. We were poor...our entertainment was walking down to a local pond to feed the ducks. But, we were happy, and that was forty-six years ago.

So, that was the "what" of our story in brief. I have thought about the "why" of it as well. Why these two people at this time? Here are my thoughts. We lived on a small base when we met. There were not a lot of eligible people around. We were older for our generation, and I guess, we were looking for an anchor. We knew each other before we began dating. I knew Fred to be a dedicated teacher. He had to do five preparations for five different high school classes. He coached two sports at once, track and tennis, driving back and forth between the two practice sites until the Base Captain sent a message to the school kindly asking him to refrain from making that trip across the golf course. He was respected and liked by the other high school teachers.

Through the dating part of our time there, we found we had many things in common: classical music, politics, history, and a love for travel. I am not sure we would have noticed each other on a dating website. It seems to me that deciding on someone to date that you cannot see in context would make it much more difficult even though the online dating commercials sell a different story. They promote a fairytale-like hype around Internet dating and what relationships should look like.

And why have we been together for forty-six years when other marriages have not fared so well? I don't think any relationship is perfect...at least very few of them are. Recently, at a meeting with a group of women who have all been married for a long time, one piped up, "Have you ever thought of divorcing your husband?" A great deal of raucous laughter erupted. There are always ups and downs in any relationship. But, I think we have always respected each other. We still have many of the same interests. We try to maintain good manners in our relationship and treat each other as politely as we would someone we don't know. We encourage each other to do the things we love even if they are not a shared interest. We are fortunate in our home life that each person carries part of the workload. We are both well aware of each other's weaknesses and peculiarities. That is the part that demands a sense of humor and the practice of "keeping one eye closed." We still travel. We still have "library dates." We loved and enjoyed our children intensely and still do.

All in all, we have worked at our relationship. All in all, we feel very fortunate that the work paid off. All in all, it has been a journey in which we created our own happiness as individuals and as a partners.

# PLAYLIST

No One Else * Amel Larrieux
Try Sleeping with a Broken Heart * Alicia Keys
Losing My Ground * Fergie
What Now * Rihanna
Try * P!nk
I'm Every Woman * Chaka Khan
Ain't No Sunshine * Emily King
Knockin' * Ledisi
Try Again * Aaliyah
Lions, Tigers & Bears * Jazmine Sullivan
Best Thing I Never Had * Beyoncé
One Is the Magic # * Jill Scott
Fading * Rihanna
Who You Are * Jessie J
Soldier of Love * Sade
Didn't Cha Know * Erykah Badu
What's My Name? * Rihanna & Drake
Never Gonna Get It * En Vogue
Deja Vu * Beyoncé feat. Jay-Z
Bruised But Not Broken * Joss Stone
Love Me Unique * Michael Franti

Va Va Voom * Nicki Minaj

Me, Myself and I * Beyoncé

Feeling Good * Nina Simone

No, No, No Part 2 * Destiny's Child feat. Wyclef Jean

There You Go * P!nk

Private Party * India.Arie

Save Me * Nicki Minaj

Sick 'n' Tired * Ms. Dynamite

Get to Know You * Ledisi

Blow Me (One Last Kiss) * P!nk

Be OK * Chrisette Michele

Tell Me Something Good * Rufus feat. Chaka Khan

You're Not the Man * Sade

No More Drama * Mary J. Blige

I Can't Make You Love Me * Adele

I Want a Little Sugar in My Bowl * Nina Simone

I Try * Macy Gray

Sugar Mama * Beyoncé

Pieces of Me * Ledisi

I Am Woman * Jordin Sparks

Breakthrough * Jazzyfatnastees

We All Want Love * Rihanna

Higher Than This * Ledisi

Krazy Krush * Ms. Dynamite

Ego * Beyoncé

I Wanna Dance with Somebody * Whitney Houston

That Good Good * Ledisi

Free Your Mind * En Vogue

Endless Love * Diana Ross & Lionel Richie

Gravity * Sara Bareilles

Strength, Courage and Wisdom * India.Arie

I Gotta Find Peace of Mind * Lauryn Hill

Next Lifetime * Erykah Badu

HEATHER ALAINE

I Used to Love Him * Lauryn Hill
Strong as Glass * Goapele
Ready for Love * India.Arie

# THANK YOU

A special shout-out to these Loves, for not only believing in me, but also investing above and beyond when this book was in its beginning cocoon phase.

Drea Estacio
Valerie Tookes
Ruth McGrath
Georgeta Masson
Alice Ann Worland
Penny Barthel
Melanie ElLaissi
Parissa Peymani
Fred and Linda Meyer
Kathy Moore
Meliza Wells Mora
Stacy Maher
Sarah Crist
Grace Yoon
Katharine Hada
Rocio Guzman
Mary Jane Weatherbee
Ellen Neumark

Inger Stark
Roxy Lo
Britt Bravo
Heather Crandall
Eleni Yatar
Krystal Shields
Gabriela Nassar Covarelli
Deborah Sherman
Alison Dunn
Jennifer Schmitz
Kristin Hull
Samar Nassar
Hilary Casey
Clien Wintzen
Hannah Pelletier
Jennifer Moore
Rose Foronda
Iris Chin
Diana Garcia
Terri Washington
Jill Linderbaum
Janet Conery
Madison Reeb
Chris and Amanda Howell
Maria Landy
Brett Meyer
Cathy Hozian Gonzalez
Christie Canaria